Laurence Sterne
and the
Origins of the Musical Novel

# Laurence Sterne
## and the Origins of the
## Musical Novel

WILLIAM FREEDMAN

The University of Georgia Press
Athens

Copyright © 1978 by the University of Georgia Press
Athens 30602

All rights reserved

Set in 12 on 14 point Garamond No. 3 type
Printed in the United States of America

Library of Congress Cataloging in Publication Data

Freedman, William.
    Laurence Sterne and the origins of the musical
novel.
    Includes bibliographical references and index.
    1. Sterne, Laurence, 1713–1768.  The life and
opinions of Tristram Shandy, gentleman.   2. Sterne,
Laurence, 1713–1768—Knowledge—Music.   3. Music and literature.   I. Title.
PR3714.T73F7            823'.6            77–7082
            ISBN 0–8203–0429–8

For Debby
and for Jennifer,
with love and praise
before and after

Early music presents many insoluble problems to those who set out to reconstruct and interpret it. In few of the problems, however, is it so hazardous to attempt any definite codex of law and practice as in that of *musica ficta*—i.e. the insertion of accidentals into a text. That composers, from the earliest times, intended such occasional modifications to be made by the performers is beyond any possible doubt: indeed the ancient name for an accidental (*signum asininum* or "ass's mark") is clear evidence that its insertion by a composer was a reflection on the competence of the singer. But there is little or no agreement among the old theorists as to the laws of interpretation; which seems to imply either that there was no unanimity in practice or that the theorists themselves suffered from the malady endemic to their tribe. For it is characteristic of all theorists to epitomize and codify the very usages which the creative minds of their contemporaries have decisively abandoned. Nor is there, at the present day, any solid agreement among the most thoughtful students of ancient music—no two of whom would, in all probability, produce an identical "fair-copy" of any given manuscript from the earliest times down to Orlando Gibbons. The most reasonable course, therefore, is to attempt to state impartially the conditions of the problem and the difficulties inherent in its solution.

"Music is called *ficta* when we make a tone to be a semitone, or, conversely, a semitone to be a tone." And the problem for the student consists in this: since the composer did not (or seldom did) tell the performer, by means of accidentals, when these changes were to be made, how could the performer know?

"Fictive Music"
(*Grove's Dictionary of Music and Musicians*)

Sister and mother and diviner love,
And of the sisterhood of the living dead
Most near, most clear, and of the clearest bloom,
And of the fragrant mothers the most dear
And queen, and of diviner love the day
And flame and summer and sweet fire, no thread
Of cloudy silver sprinkles in your gown
Its venom of renown, and on your head
No crown is simpler than the simple hair.

Now, of the music summoned by the birth
That separates us from the wind and sea,
Yet leaves us in them, until earth becomes,
By being so much of the things we are,
Gross effigy and simulacrum, none
Gives motion to perfection more serene
Than yours, out of our imperfections wrought,
Most rare, or ever of more kindred air
In the laborious weaving that you wear.

For so retentive of themselves are men
That music is intensest which proclaims
The near, the clear, and vaunts the clearest bloom,
And of all vigils musing the obscure,
That apprehends the most which sees and names,
As in your name, an image that is sure,
Among the arrant spices of the sun,
O bough and bush and scented vine, in whom
We give ourselves our likest issuance.

Yet not too like, yet not so like to be
Too near, too clear, saving a little to endow
Our feigning with the strange unlike, whence springs
The difference that heavenly pity brings.
For this, musician, in your girdle fixed
Bear other perfumes. On your pale head wear
A band entwining, set with fatal stones.
Unreal, give back to us what once you gave:
The imagination that we spurned and crave.

Wallace Stevens,
"To the One of Fictive Music"

# Contents

# 1

## Introduction: Music and Fiction

All art may not constantly aspire to the condition (or structure or effects) of music, but a substantial body of nineteenth- and twentieth-century fiction does. André Gide, in 1925, was perhaps the first major novelist to declare and detail his interest in the systematic use of music as a structural model—the "musicalization of fiction," as Huxley was to name it—but Gide was by no means either the first or the last to attempt it. Thomas Mann, who confessed to a "deep inward affinity" for music, spoke comfortably of the "musical affinities" of *Tonio Kröger* (a work that has been quite persuasively analyzed as a literary sonata)[1] and employed a variety of musical techniques in *The Magic Mountain* and *Buddenbrooks* as well, notably thematic development and the Wagnerian leitmotiv. It was in *Tonio Kröger*, Mann wrote in 1936, that "I first learned to employ music as a shaping influence in my art. The conception of epic-associations, I later on largely employed in *The Magic Mountain*."[2] Similar motives led Proust to the use of "symphonic" principles of thematic development and interplay in *Remembrance of Things Past*, the first volume of which, *Swann's Way*, begins with an "overture." In *L'Héroique* (1921) and *La Pastorale* (1924), the French novelist Paul Emile Cadilhac produced examples of what he called the "symphonic novel," taking its shape and special character from the fugal, motivic, and variational development of themes and creating, as he put it, "a musical atmosphere by the use of images, comparisons, and words borrowed from the musical vocabulary."[3] Hermann Hesse strove for a simultaneous "double-voiced melody and eternally moving antithesis" in *Der Kurgast* and described his *Steppenwolf* as a sonata built around the "intermezzo" of "The Treatise."[4] Huxley's *Point Counter Point* is a confessed experiment in literary modulation, variation, and counterpoint. Gide repeatedly described himself as "a musician" and *The Counterfeiters* as a musical, principally a fugal composition.[5] The sirens section of *Ulysses*, one of the most familiar and successful ventures in the direction of literary fugue, though by no means the only one, is but one aspect of the pervasive musical experimentalism of *Ulysses* and *Finnegans Wake*.[6] Both novels are rich in contrapuntal and variational techniques, and *Ulysses*, taken as a whole, has been variously labelled both a literary sonata and (more modestly and plausibly) a symphonic poem.[7]

This brief list could easily be stretched to several times its length, but only tedium would be served. "What I should like to do," announces Edouard in *The Counterfeiters*, "is something like the art of fugue writing. And I cannot see why what was possible in music should be impossible in literature."[8] Whether or not the musically possible is transferable to literature, Edouard articulates the ambition not only of André Gide but of an impressive and growing number of novelists. The effort, whatever its difficulties and perhaps partly because of them, is clearly an intriguing one, no less common to modern fiction than important to its development.

The systematic "musicalization" of poetry and fiction is usually traced back to the German romantic poets of the early nineteenth century and the French symbolists half a century later, both quite explicit and eloquent if not always shatteringly lucid in explaining their practice. The matter is complicated, but basically, German romantic poets like Tieck, Wackenroder, and Hoffman turned to music for its fluidity and transience and for its capacity to bring harmony and order out of abundance and dissonance. Speech merely reckons, names, and describes in a foreign material the "mysterious stream in the depths of the human spirit." Only music "streams it out before us as it is in itself." And only music "reduces the most manifold and most contradictory movements of our soul to the same beautiful harmonies."[9]

The French symbolists—mainly Valéry, Mallarmé and Redon—also brought music to poetry for its unique capacity to represent the evanescence and harmonize the dissonant affluence of the inner life. But two other factors multiplied its attraction: its formal autonomy and its indefinite, reverberative suggestiveness. Art, for the symbolists, was not primarily an imitation of the external world, but a bounded world in itself, a "globed compacted thing," in Virginia Woolf's phrase. A poem, for Mallarmé, is a "geometry of phrases," a complex system of "reciprocal reflections," yet at the same time infinitely suggestive and suggestive of infinity. It was, to update the metaphor, a kind of geodesic dome radiant of eternity; and music, exonerated from denotative reference to the world, an enclosed formal system of suggestive sound in expressive motion, was again the model of the arts.

The German romantics and the French symbolists were the first to theorize in any systematic way about the role of music in their work. But nearly half a century before the former, a full century before the latter, and a hundred and fifty years before the stream-of-consciousness novel began to take its musical shape, Laurence Sterne, anticipating their preoccupation with the inner life and the problems of transience, diversity, and dissonance it raises, and anticipating many of their attitudes toward both literature and music, likewise anticipated their experiments and solutions.

Sterne was an innovator and a remarkably fertile one. Almost all of his major experiments in subject and form took root and reemerged, after more than a century of almost total neglect, in the modern novel, particularly the lyrical (or symbolic) and psychological novels.

The subordination of narrative plot to the presentation of a private inner world; the use of object and experience primarily as brush-strokes in a psychological self-portrait; the preoccupation with the complex interrelationships between inner and outer world and the inevitable subjective transformation of "reality"; the concern with psychological time or duration rather than clock time, and the sense of time as an all-pervading present that includes past and future rather than as an orderly procession of separate events; the concern with simultaneity and the flow of consciousness, with "the process of living," "life caught in the very act of being," and the search for a form to express and objectify that flux—these are the characteristic preoccupations of the Bergsonian psychological novels of Joyce and Virginia Woolf, of Proust and André Gide, and all are found and richly developed in *Tristram Shandy*. Beyond this, the search for an appropriate form brought Sterne to the time-shift technique more than a century and a half before the implications and influence of Henri Bergson and William James made antichronology almost standard literary fare. And the juggling of time is but part of a wider complex of calculated dissolution and reintegration that is a differentiating mark of *Tristram Shandy* and of modern experimental fiction. "The confused chronology, the complicated system of cross-references, the erratic syntax and the eccentric development of language are all part of the method that Virginia Woolf consciously adopted"[10] and that others have incorporated with less awareness perhaps, but no smaller debt.

Nor is this all. As René Wellek and Austin Warren point out, Sterne is the founder of the romantic-ironic mode of epic narration, one that "deliberately magnifies the role of the narrator, delights in violating any possible illusion that this is 'life' and not 'art'; [and] emphasizes the written literary character of the book." The line begins with Sterne, runs through the work of Jean Paul Richter and Ludwig Tieck in Germany, of Veltman and Gogol in Russia, more recently through Gide's *The Counterfeiters* and Huxley's *Point Counter Point*,[11] down to contemporary fiction. Sterne wrote a novel about writing a novel and opened a door experimental novelists have been walking through ever since.

The list of Sterne's contributions to the art of fiction is formidable. Robert Gorham Davis put the case accurately and succinctly when he observed that "*Tristram Shandy* demonstrates more fully and translucently the basic ontology of the novel, the sense of what the novel really is and does, as we have come to understand it in recent decades, than any modern novel you can mention, no matter in what particular respects that other novel may have gone beyond *Tristram Shandy*."[12] Virginia Woolf's observation of some fifty years ago is hardly less true today: Sterne is indeed "singularly of our age"; and the point I want to make is that much of what Sterne's novel is and does and much of what modern fiction has derived from him is distinctively musical in character. Sterne's principal concerns and contributions are in the realms of time, process, the flow of consciousness, communication, and form; and each of these facets of his fertile originality is inseparable from yet another: the transmutation of musical rhetoric, principles, and structure to literature.

Although Sterne's was a profoundly personal, even idiosyncratic precocity, history had a predictably strong and active hand in it. Sterne's adult life coincides not only with the first stirrings of the romanticism that extolled music as the model of the arts and aspired to its "condition," but with a burgeoning movement to somehow unite the arts in general, poetry and music in particular.

Associationalism, analyzed by Locke in his *Essay Concerning Human Understanding* (1690) and elaborated and formalized in David Hartley's *Observations on Man* (1749), exerted a powerful influence not only on the synaesthetic poetry of the following century, but more immediately on the contemporary view of the relationship between the arts. The doctrine eroded the barrier first between thought and feeling, then between sensations and the emotions they give rise to. After midcentury, associationists began serious inquiry into the emotional interconnectedness of sight, sound, and touch, and Edmund Burke articulated a familiar conclusion when he proclaimed, "There is a chain in all our sensations; they are all but different sorts of feeling calculated to be affected by various sorts of objects, but all to be affected after the same manner." [13] One of the consequences of this concept of a chain-relationship among the senses was a growing belief in the unified affectivity of the arts. They were, as Christof Gluck observed, interchangeable; what could be expressed by one art form could be expressed by another: music, like poetry, could be "picturesque"; the pictorial, whether in nature or painting, might elicit responses more typically associated with music or poetry; and music numbered among its most significant powers its capacity to deepen and enrich poetic meaning by embellishing the spoken word.

All the arts, then, were in some sense interchangeable; though they reached us through different sense organs, they provoked similar effects. But there were special affinities, a special intimacy, between the arts of poetry and music. By the end of the seventeenth century the doctrine of the affections, emphasizing music's capacity to "move the affections or excite passion," as Descartes put it, had all but completely replaced the older explanations of music's powers.[14] The power of music was no longer traced primarily to its special status as the aesthetic model of universal harmony—cosmological, social, and psychological—but to its capacity to "strike upon the passions." The principal cause of this altered focus was the gradual shift from the mimetic to the expressive theory of music and to its concomitant and deepening association with the art of rhetoric. "The goddess PERSUASION," wrote Shaftesbury, "must have been in a manner the mother of poetry, rhetoric, music, and the other kindred arts."[15] And as children of the same parent—"sister arts" as they were called—music and poetry bore the closest blood relationship to one another. Persuasion was principally emotive, the rhetorical force of both arts a function of their common emotive power, but theorists like Vico, Rousseau, Monboddo, and John Brown gave music precedence and place. Anticipating Otto Jespersen's observation that "men sang out their feelings long before they were able to

speak their thought,"[16] they claimed that music antedated
poetry and speech as an expression of human passion and
surpassed it in intensity.

Music was the language of the passions in its purest form,
"a new magical language of the feelings," as Herder wrote
of ancient music. Although it "speaks by means of mere
sensations without concepts, and so does not, like poetry,
leave anything over for reflection, it yet moves the mind in
a greater variety of ways and more intensely, although only
transitorily."[17] But this was less a competition than an opportunity for cooperation in a return to the original condition of mutual dependency. The doctrine of association
testified that both music and speech derived much of their
emotive potency from their mutual association with the
feelings they expressed, and each could only be strengthened
and deepened by a connection with the other. Herder,
among others, looked forward to a merger of the arts where
the maximum of expression would be achieved with minimal conflict between the idiosyncratic qualities of each, an
ideal union between a new poetry and a new music.[18]
Herder's dream was Wagner's achievement, but it was left
to Sterne—novelist, viola da gambist, and a man of original
parts—to seek a different kind of union, to merge language
with music in quite another and less familiar way and in so
doing to lay the foundation and begin the development of
an important new technique for fiction. History will help,
but it will not account. The conducive context was there,
but the leap to Sterne's performance was a long one. The
unique voice alarms us still.

Experiments in aesthetic synthesis were not confined to
music and poetry. Father Castel, a French priest, constructed
a color clavichord (ancestor of the modern color organ)

equating colors with the notes of the scale via "common" associations—*do* and blue with majesty, *re* and green with a rural sprightliness, etc.[19] The romantic poets of the next century used synaesthetic imagery with similar but more sensible intent. And the effort culminated in the massive multimedia synthesis of Wagnerian opera, placing nearly equal stress on music, drama, text, and scene and fusing them into a single multiplex form.

A comparable if more modest fusion is evident in *Tristram Shandy*, a novel rich not only in musical metaphors and techniques, but in dramatic and portraitive ones as well. The book is shot through with meticulously detailed descriptions of posture and gesture strongly reminiscent of stage directions and with metaphors calling attention to the dramatic character of Sterne's book. Tristram makes frequent reference to the "heroes" on "the stage of this dramatic work," and periodically brings down the "curtain" on one "scene" in order to open it on another. Painting and the graphic arts are equally well represented. The normal printed pages of the work are broken by illustrative diagrams and pointing hands and separated by a black page mourning the death of Yorick, a marbled page ("motley emblem of my work"), and a blank page on which the reader is invited to draw the Widow Wadman according to the lights of his own fancy. And the graphic element, like the dramatic, is underscored by pertinent metaphors, surprisingly appropriate references to the "drawing" of character, the "familiar strokes and faint designations of it," the "outline," "colouring," and "composition" of his mock dedication, the "foreground" and "background" of his work, and so on. If one is looking for analogies this early on, perhaps opera is appropriate. It does at least reasonable justice to the synaesthetic atmosphere of the work and the richness of interaesthetic interplay and design.

Sterne's critics and biographers have been neither blind nor deaf to the synaesthetic quality of *Tristram Shandy*, sensing if not a serious attempt to reunify the arts, at least an occasional inclination to blend them, to incorporate into his work metaphors, devices, and effects traditionally associated with the other arts, even, some have suggested, to model his writing after them.[20] Everyone, of course, has his favorite vehicle (as I have mine), but music, it seems to me, has been given the poorest ride. Not that it has not been noticed—it has, and often[21]—but because it can be taken so much farther than the others and so much farther than it has been allowed to go.

Sterne was an artificer. His effort in *Tristram Shandy* is an effort to both represent and transcend life through art. For Sterne, the distinction between life and art is but another in the endless run of impossible distinctions both art and life try to force upon us. On the one hand, art is not life but art, Tristram's book not life but a creative effort whose progress—or lack of it—we are invited to witness. From one point of view, then, art may transcend life, and the end product is not an imitation of an action, not a narrative autobiography, but an esthetic design, an artificial world with a life and realities of its own. All the references to the art of creation and to other art forms—to painting, drama, and music—deepen our sense of the novel as creation. It is painted. It is staged. It is composed. To transcend life, however, is not to escape it. It is merely to turn inward to another life, the life that creates life, the life of mind and feeling. Given that, the portraits and the stage are aspects of the external world of the novel. Tristram paints his figures, directs his drama, manages his stage. But this is all, as it were, only part of the act. These are but the props he is working with—the ideas, themes, tools, and counters that are the materials from which Sterne (or Tristram) creates his musical design. They are the matter set in motion in the mechanical world of the novel, but it is the motion itself that reflects the more important inner life of the protagonist, and the motion is musical. The world of *Tristram Shandy* is an artificial world, but the artifice is real just as surely as art has life. The artifice is a complex of musical patterns, but musical patterns, as we shall see, are also the forms and movements of that other reality, the human mind. Music, in other words, is more than just another element in the composition of the artifice. It is at the heart of the novel.

The "musical novel" Sterne fathered is a branch of what Ralph Freedman defines as the "lyrical novel" in his very useful book by that name.[22] Conditioned by the increased interest in psychology, by the growing emphasis on mood and feeling, and by the Kantian reconciliation of inner and outer worlds, early nineteenth-century playwrights and novelists abandoned the traditional emphasis on narrative plot in favor of an interior portrait of the transforming self. Object and event are subordinated to imagery and portraiture under the pressure of the protagonist's reformation of the external world into a texture of imagery, a complex of musical and pictorial patterns, a formal aesthetic design uniting self and world.

While acknowledging *Tristram Shandy*'s influence on the subsequent development of the lyrical novel, Freedman is doubtful of its status. Without specifying which, he finds it "lacking in many of the characteristics of lyrical technique," principally, it seems, unity of design. Whether or not one ultimately decides to classify *Tristram Shandy* as "lyrical fiction" is a moot point, but the source of Freedman's own hesitation is instructive. When he questions the unity of the novel's design and all but disqualifies it as a kind of "patchwork quilt," he reveals the strong pictorial emphasis of the genre as he defines it. While the total design of the lyrical novel may and often does include musical patterns of thematic development, what emerges in the end is a "texture of imagery," a pattern of woven tapestry, self-portraiture. The basic tension that animates the form stems from the contrast and interaction between imagistic design and linear narrative. In *Tristram Shandy*, on the other hand, and in many later "musical novels," the tension arises out of the conflict between two potentially contradictory modes of progression: the narrative and the musical. And what happens in *Tristram Shandy* points to an important distinction between the musical and lyrical novels, or perhaps more accurately to a set of related differentiae. The emphasis in musical fiction is on process. In the lyrical novel the "lyrical process," which may include musical patterns of development, is a means subordinate to the ends of landscape and portraiture, and a contributory part of a unified and basically pictorial aesthetic design. In *Tristram Shandy* and in much of the musical fiction that follows from or after it, the stress is on the process itself. *Tristram Shandy* is not a patchwork quilt but the weave of its threads, and Sterne is more interested in *how* one goes about looking than in what one sees, more interested in the act of weaving or the directions of the weave than in the tapestry that emerges. Narration, consequently, is subordinated not to any "aesthetic design," where "aesthetic" means sensually appealing and purposely ordered and unified, but more specifically to the various principles and designs which generate and shape musical composition: contrapuntal interplay, theme and variation, repetition and recapitulation, modulation, concentricity, and so on. The emphasis is not on the primarily spatial experience of time, on Pound's "exploded image" ("an emotional and intellectual complex in an instant of time"), but rather on process and progression, on fluid patterns of temporal simultaneity and flow, the subtle ooze or violent shifts of thought and feeling—on the working image not exploded but repeatedly exploding.

If the distinguishing mark of the lyrical novel is "portraiture, the halting of the rush of time within constellations of images or figures,"[23] the mark of the musical novel is, naturally enough, music; and the aim is not to halt time in patterns of imagery, but somehow to reproduce its insistent flow in moving patterns of narrative, memory, and thought. To sum up briefly what should emerge from the following chapters, the lyrical novel is likely to take a distinctively musical turn: (1) when it is preoccupied with either or both of the principal problems of time—simultaneity and evanescence; (2) when its forms or subject matter include the various movements and patterns of consciousness paralleled by the patterns of musical motion: counterpoint, theme and variation, thematic development, repetition, and so on; (3) when it is no less concerned with apprehension than comprehension and strives for an evocation of feelings and effects traditionally associated with music: ineffability, evanescence and rapid change, harmoniousness, and so on; (4) when its effort, as in Hesse, Tieck, and Sterne, is to bring aesthetic harmony out of the multiple vacillations, dissonances, and contradictions of human activity, thought, and feeling.

Categorizing *Tristram Shandy* is like crating wishes. It is a lyrical novel, a dramatic novel, a symbolic novel, a romantic-ironic novel, and "some might even question whether it can properly be called a novel at all; though if not a novel it would surely be hard to decide in what technical category of writing it ought to be placed."[24] John Cowper Powys's doubts are well taken, and the wisest course might be simply to let the matter stand and turn to more important questions of language, subject, form, influence, and effect. I am rejecting that course here, suggesting that *Tristram Shandy* is (not exclusively, but additionally, perhaps primarily) a musical novel precisely because viewing Sterne's elusive book from that perspective can help us answer these more urgent questions and can help us raise and at least deal with still broader questions of music, literature, and the possible connections between them. A full-length study of the role of music in *Tristram Shandy* will, I hope, serve several complementary and useful purposes.

One is simply biographical—to suggest at least the strong possibility that music was an important component not only of Sterne's prose style and metaphoric imagination, but of his structural—indeed in the broadest sense "creative"— imagination as well, that it governed, whether by choice or mere seepage, his choice of language, tone, rhythms, metaphors, but above all his sense of process and design. I want to suggest, in other, riskier words, that in effect Sterne heard music in his head while he wrote *Tristram Shandy*, that the styles, forms, techniques, and rhythms of the music he played and heard so often worked their way—perhaps irresistibly, perhaps by cordial invitation—into his novel. Important biographical data gives credence to these claims. Sterne was a dedicated and habitual concertgoer and subscriber and counted among his friends a number of musicians and music-lovers, chief among them two of his most ardent flirtations, the professional singers Catherine Fourmantel and Elizabeth Vesey.[25] But by far the most pertinent biographical fact is that Sterne was for most of his life a practicing musician, at least a competent and perhaps an accomplished gambist.

There are a number of references to his "fiddling" in Sterne's letters[26] and in contemporary anecdotes about him, but more important is the nature of the instrument he fiddled on, the kind of music written for it, and the conventions of its performance. Through most of the sixteenth and seventeenth centuries, and, in England, through part of the eighteenth as well, the viola da gamba was *the* instrument of virtuosity, used extensively for "embroidering a bass with brilliant runs, arpeggios, and other embellishments" and for building up "a polyphonic structure out of its own resources."[27] The viola da gamba lends itself admirably to rich "chords and music in parts, as well as to rapid and brilliant divisions. In the high register, beyond the frets, it can do all the tricks of expression of the violin, and with as free a tone. . . . Furthermore, a continual variety of effects was devised from varied tunings of which there were many."[28] The implications of these descriptions for *Tristram Shandy* are striking, and I want to deal with them, but the immediate point is simply that the gambist in Sterne's time took on a far weightier theoretical task than his contemporary counterpart. The modern cellist, for example, can hope for respectability as an instrumentalist, primarily on the strength of technical craftsmanship. A solid grounding in music theory and composition is desirable, of course, essential for real musicianship and genuine mastery; but one can "play" his instrument and play it quite well, if he knows his craft. Two hundred years ago, instrumentalists, perhaps keyboard players and gambists above all, had a much harder time of it. Since improvisation (often on an extremely rudimentary score) was among the gambist's principal tasks, every player was expected at the same time to be at least one part composer; and if he was to function at all—not necessarily brilliantly, but minimally—he required some knowledge of division and other improvisational techniques, of chordal and melodic relationships, of harmony and tonality, of polyphony, cadential formuli, and so on. He needed, in short, at least a working knowledge of music theory and composition; and treatises like Christopher Simpson's *The Division Viol* (1659), providing detailed procedural instruction, were required reading. Simpson's book was no mere performer's handbook, but "a dignified school of improvisation and of all the forms in which that art was exercised."[29] It was also the classic instruction book for English string players, and it is all but unthinkable that Sterne was not familiar with it, with other treatises of its kind, and with the improvisatory techniques and rationales they taught.

The biographical generates, if it does not include, a second purpose, structural and analogical: to suggest, indifferent to intention, that there are analogies, often striking, between the principles of order and rational structure in *Tristram Shandy* on the one hand, and principles and patterns of musical structure and design on the other. The application of these analogies is useful, I think, for bringing order out of the primeval ooze, for taming the flooding tide of experience the novel threatens to drown and drown us in; and whether the design is in some sense actually *in* the work or is superimposed, grid-fashion, as an instrument of explanation and description is perhaps no more resolvable than a similar question asked of hypotheses about the composition of light. The only fruitful test is how much it explains, how accurately it describes.

Although this kind of description has its own intrinsic worth, there is nothing comparable to prediction when we are speaking of the arts, and there my analogy with physical theories breaks down. It is well to know what is going on in a work of art. The worth of the effort is in some kind of proportionate relation to the worth of the object, and anything that illuminates a valued object acquires a small measure of borrowed value for itself. But the measure is, at least potentially, small indeed. Unless the musicality of the work in some way relates to the literary life of the novel and contributes to effect, its explication like its presence becomes a mere show of virtuosity. One of the points I hope will emerge from this study—its third purpose—is that this is not true of the musicality of *Tristram Shandy*. I want to suggest that some of the novel's most prominent and mystifying effects, like its puzzling principles of order, disorder, and design, are those traditionally associated more with musical than with literary composition and that they derive, in part at least, from the same source. *Tristram Shandy* is no mere frigate out of mutton bones. It floats.

A fourth aim is historical, perhaps literary-genetic: to press and validate a claim for Sterne as the first author to bring musical techniques and patterns to fiction on a major scale and, at the same time, to strengthen and broaden the foundation for the claim that he stands first in the ever-lengthening line of authors of what might be called the patterned novel or the novel as pliable urn. The patterned novel would include what Thomas Mann calls the "epic prose-composition as a weaving of themes, as a musical complex of associations"; but it would also include those stream-of-consciousness novels whose potential plunge into chaos is checked only by the interweaving of "a pattern almost free of representation." And it would include too Robbe-Grillet's "ontic duplicate," the lyrical or symbolist novel that "depends less upon sequence of events than upon reflexive relationships among its elements," and David Grossvogel's novel as ritual, all of which exist less as mimesis than as pattern, phenomenological samples "as alien and as familiar as any other within the phenomenal world."[30] This is the novel as malleable urn, more artifact than container, but container as well as artifact, and one whose shape is necessarily identical with the materials it holds. It is the novel aiming, as Thomas Mann put it, "always and consistently *to be* that of which it speaks."

One final point in what begins to look suspiciously like a Shandean chapter on purposes: The parallels and analogues, I hope, may help us understand a little more about the common ground between music and literature—about the way authors often imitate, adapt, or simply duplicate musical processes, at the very least about some of the ways they might if they are so inclined, and, more generally and joyfully, about the surprising unity of the arts.

# 2

## Form, Content, and the Process of Mind

---

### *Rules Adapted to the Subject*

In a now famous letter to Dr. John Eustace, Sterne took up
the doctor's analogy between an odd walking stick the
doctor had sent him and *Tristram Shandy* and replied in the
following way: "Your walking stick is in no sense more
*shandaic* than in that of its having *more handles than one*—
The parallel breaks only in this, that in using the stick,
every one will take the handle which suits his convenience.
In Tristram Shandy, the handle is taken which suits their
passions, their ignorance or sensibility."[1] The remark is
prophetic. The history of the criticism of this book has indeed been a history of handle-grabbing, and there seem to
have been very nearly as many handles as critics. Some have
taken hold of the book's "sentimentalism," others its "ob-
scenity." Some have called attention to the curious prose
style, others to the characterization; some to the unique
blend of humor and pathos, others to the rhetoric. Some
critics have stressed the Newtonian influence, others the
Lockean; some the Humean, still others the Shaftesburean;
and as one rare handleless (merely multihandled?) critic
observed, it can also be interpreted in the light of Freudian
psychology, Camusian existentialism, and even Dalian sur-
realism.[2]

But no facet of this prismatic novel has been more closely

or more frequently scrutinized than its mystifying structure
—or lack of one. The writer for the *Critical Review* spoke
for most of Sterne's contemporaries when he called *Tristram Shandy* a work "which seems to have been written
without any plan, or any other design than that of chewing
the author's wit, humour, and learning, in an unconnected
effusion of sentiments and remarks, thrown out indiscrimi-
nately as they rose in his imagination." Oliver Goldsmith
and Horace Walpole agreed. Goldsmith wryly reduced the
book to "nine hundred and ninety-five breaks, seventy-two
ha ha's, three good things, and a caster"; while Walpole
called it a "very insipid and tedious performance . . . a
kind of novel . . . the great humour of which consists in the
whole narration always going backwards."[3]

This view did not die with the eighteenth century. The
dominant reaction of the nineteenth is epitomized in Walter
Bagehot's scorn for the "fantastic disorder of the form,"
for its lack of plan or order which rendered it, in Bagehot's
mind, "in every generation unfit for analysis." And the
same judgment, in more tolerant form, persists into the
present century. "Obviously a god is hidden in *Tristram
Shandy*," remarked E. M. Forster, "his name is Muddle, and
some readers cannot accept him."[4]

Despite the perseverence of this attitude, the history of
the criticism of *Tristram Shandy* has been a gradual awaken-
ing to the method in Sterne's apparent madness. Critics
have come at last to the realization that something more
than felicitous vagary holds the book together and makes
it work. William Pepys, one of the first to discern traces of
order in the novel, remarked that although it is "a strange eccentric composition," yet "it could be tried by rules adapted

to the subject, & a judgment pronounced upon its merits."
Since Pepys's acute observation in 1776, Sterne's more sympathetic critics have been trying to do precisely that, but the
problem has been to discover just what rules are, in fact,
adapted to this very puzzling subject. In other words, until
quite recently, the growing willingness to admit the presence of rational order in *Tristram* has been unaccompanied
by any agreement about the nature of the ordering principle. For William Enfield, a critic for the *Monthly Review*,
"Sterne's originality did not consist in a want of method":
the true "Shandyan manner" was a "conversation-style without its defects." About a half century later, in what was
easily the keenest and most constructive analysis of Sterne
to date, Coleridge attributed the cohesion of the novel to
the pervasive presence of its dramatically contrasted characters. In our own century, Theodore Baird has called attention to the chronological sequence that anchors the erratic
surface; Wilbur Cross, James Work, and Samuel Monk
have championed Locke's doctrine of the association of ideas
as the cohesive principle; while John Traugott maintains
that on the contrary *Tristram* is a parody of Locke's doctrines, not an embodiment, and that the whole is held together by Sterne's rhetoric. The novel, says Traugott, is
"a studied relentless burlesque of rhetorical techniques by
which he writes a history of the mind in terms of constantly
conflicting attitudes."[5]

This last suggestion points the way to something akin to
agreement in recent criticism, but the agreement is of a very
general kind, and the difficulty readers have had and con-
tinue to have with the structure of *Tristram Shandy* is largely a result of the general failure to "try" it by the appro-

priate rules. The rules adapted to the subject have gone
unused because they are not usually appropriate to this
subject at all, not usually suited to literature, certainly not
to the novel, least of all to the early English novel. They
are rules appropriate to, becaused derived from, music.

Tristram Shandy, author, assumes two quite contradictory
stances on the question of order and deliberate composition.
In one he is the devil-may-care rambler who pursues his
own whims and impulses wherever they may lead him, the
man who does "all things out of all rule" and who follows
"no man's rule who ever lived":

> A sudden impulse comes across me——drop the curtain, *Shandy*
> ——I drop it——Strike a line here across the paper, *Tristram*
> ——I strike it——and hey for a new chapter!
>     The duce of any other rule have I to govern myself by in this
> affair——and if I had one——as I do all things out of all rule——I
> would twist it and tear it to pieces, and throw it into the fire when
> I had done——Am I warm? I am, and the cause demands it——a
> pretty story! is a man to follow rules——or rules to follow him? [6]

At other times, however, Tristram is almost equally insistent that all is not impulse and accident: "if I should seem
now and then to trifle upon the road,——or should sometimes put on a fool's cap with a bell to it, for a moment or
two as we pass along,——don't fly off,——but rather
courteously give me credit for a little more wisdom than
appears upon my outside" (1:6.11). [7]

Both attitudes strongly suggest the musical character of
Sterne's creation. Let's begin with the second: Tristram's
contention that despite the seeming madness he knows what
he is about.

## *More Wisdom Than Appears*

During one of his recurrent moments of authorial self-consciousness, Tristram explains his omission of a certain chapter on the grounds that, however good it may be, its inclusion would have destroyed

> that necessary equipoise and balance, (whether of good or bad) betwixt chapter and chapter, from whence the just proportions and harmony of the whole work results. . . . In my opinion, to write a book is for all the world like humming a song——be but in tune with yourself, madam, 'tis no matter how high or how low you take it.
>
> ——This is the reason, may it please your reverences, that some of the lowest and flattest compositions pass off very well. (4:25.315)

Here, in the form of a summary analogy with music, is the claim he repeatedly makes elsewhere: that it is the balance, the equipoise, the harmony that counts, and that his book, if it seems to conform to no other accepted conventions of literary composition, is at least consistent and harmonious with itself.[8]

It may be, of course, that Tristram merely uses the music analogy for its convenient applicability. In eighteenth-century aesthetics music, after all, was the prototype of all harmony—cosmic, social, and emotional. But the metaphors and analogies Sterne drew from music are often less incidental and automatic, more calculated and meaningful, than they initially appear. Metaphor reinforces metaphor, deepening analogy, and Tristram reinforces his claim about harmonic composition with another music-simile that makes a similar point. His description of Walter Shandy's ritualized transition of attitude is broken by an interjection that illuminates his own narrative technique: "Attitudes are

nothing, madam,———'tis the transition from one attitude
to another———like the preparation and resolution of the
discord into harmony, which is all in all" (4:6.276–77).
In both of these explicitly musical analogies Sterne stresses
the peculiarly self-contained character of his book. The
attitudes are nothing; the transitions are all in all. How
high or low an author takes his book is of no consequence;
it need only be in tune with itself. The world of *Tristram
Shandy* is a world unto itself, a world of process and harmonious relation, and Tristram demands that his book be
read, scrutinized, and evaluated on the basis of its own compositional integrity with a minimum of reference to the
world outside it.

It is now widely conceded that the principle of formal
order in the novel, the hub of the seemingly rimless wheel,
is the mind of its narrator. As Wayne Booth puts it, *"Tristram Shandy* is the mad kind of book it seems because of the
life and opinions of the man it is about." The dramatized
narrator "has ceased here to be distinguishable from what
he relates. James's ideal of a seamless web of subject and
treatment has somehow been stumbled upon more than a
century before its time—and in a work that gives an air of
complete disorganization!"[9] Similarly, for Alan McKillop,
Sterne, like Locke, has written " 'a history-book . . . of what
passes in a man's own mind.' "

His frustrations and approximations produce comedy, dramatize
the problem of knowledge and communication, show the limitations of formal rhetoric, traditional learning, and scholarship, and
even of the new science and of language itself, and thus set forth
the general human situation. In some such way as this it seems
possible to correlate the form, the purpose, and the content of
*Tristram Shandy*.[10]

In a very real sense, the form of *Tristram Shandy* is at the same time the subject or content of the novel; it is what the novel is about. It is this internal identity that justifies Tristram's insistence on being in tune with himself and that makes his book so peculiarly self-reflexive. To put it dangerously, there is a fusion of form and content in *Tristram Shandy.* This is easily enough said and in fact is said more and more often and casually about more and more novels. But it is a precarious maxim at best, a truism at worst, and at all events no very easy formula to explain.

The identity of form and content in *Tristram Shandy* goes beyond Mark Schorer's classic formulation in "Technique as Discovery."[11] In this now traditional sense, form and content are said to be one in a work of art because the subject or content as presented through technique, as a manifestation of certain unavoidable artistic selections and decisions, is something quite different from what it would have been apart from that form or particular technique of presentation. Form, in other words, so thoroughly transforms and even creates content that one cannot profitably or even legitimately discuss either form or content as separate or separable entities.

For Schorer, technique is a wide, inclusive term. It is "really what T. S. Eliot means by 'convention'—any selection, structure, or distortion, any form or rhythm imposed upon the world of action; by means of which—it should be added—our apprehension of the world of action is enriched or renewed. In this sense, everything is technique which is not the lump of experience itself." Primarily, however, it is a matter of language and perspective, "the uses to which language, as language, is put to express the quality of experience in question; and the uses of point of view not only as a mode of dramatic delineation, but more particularly, of th matic definition." [12] By these standards, one would be hard put to name a novel where integration of technique and subject is more pervasive or complete, where subject is more tightly bound to technique or technique more determinative of substance. One can imagine, say, *Tom Jones* written in the first person, *Moll Flanders* in third, Fielding's novel in the reportorial language of Defoe, Defoe's in Fielding's elegant Augustanese. It is not a nice thing to do to one's imagination, but once the mind passes the initial shock it can manage the transformation. Both novels would be radically transformed, of course, would be very different literary animals than they are—that is precisely Schorer's point— but something, rather a good deal in fact, of the subject, the content, theme, the "lump of experience" and the meanings it carries, would remain. Now try to imagine *Tristram Shandy* written in the third person, by an omniscient narrator! And then replace that language, that frantic, pulsating, fragmentary, dash-ridden prose with someone else's (with Austen's, or with Hemingway's perhaps!), and ask what is left of subject. The most gluttonous imaginations have their limits. The thing, as Tristram would say, cannot be done. Change the language and point of view of *Tristram Shandy* and you do not merely change *Tristram Shandy*; you throw it away and write another book altogether. Content and form, subject and technique, simply will not separate and survive. This, we know from Schorer, holds for all genuine literature worthy the name, but it is more emphatically and decisively descriptive of *Tristram Shandy*. It is the difference between lobotomy and cremation.

This is one aspect of the fusion, but there is another. In

Sterne's book the identity of form and subject is a more complex matter still, and every facet of its complexity points back to the musicality of the novel as Sterne himself defines it—to the related emphases on process and on internal cohesiveness and self-containment. The fusion is more nearly complete, even if (perhaps because) we begin with greater distance between the elements headed for collision. We may allow, for argument's sake, a distinction between form and content, between what the work is about—the abstractable, paraphraseable content—and the way that content is rendered. And we are brought up short by the recognition that in *Tristram Shandy* the content, what the work is about, is in large part exactly the same as the way it is rendered, for the very simple reason that the way it is rendered is in large part precisely what it is about.

What *Tristram Shandy* is finally about is the operation of the mind of man, at least one man, and the form or seeming formlessness of the book is both result and embodiment of those mental operations. The relationship is further complicated by the fact that much of Tristram's mental effort is directed toward a confrontation with the difficulties, even impossibilities, inherent in his uncommon autobiographical task:

I am this month one whole year older than I was this time twelve-month; and having got, as you perceive, almost into the middle of my fourth volume——and no farther than to my first day's life——'tis demonstrative that I have three hundred and sixty-four days more life to write just now, than when I first set out; so that instead of advancing, as a common writer, in my work with what I have been doing at it——on the contrary, I am just thrown so many volumes back——was every day of my life to be as busy a day as this——And why not?——and the transactions and opinions of it to take up as much description——And for what reason should they be cut short? as at this rate I should just live 364 times faster than I should write——It must follow, an' please your worships, that the more I write, the more I shall have to write—— and consequently, the more your worships read, the more your worships will have to read. (4:13.285–86)

The problem of writing his book is of such concern to Tristram that he devotes no fewer than one-fifth of the chapters to it and an even higher percentage of pages.[13] Like Joyce, Proust, Huxley, Mann, and Gide—indeed like almost every writer of "musicalized" fiction—Sterne is fascinated with the act of creation. Tristram cannot take his mind off it and insists on our sharing his obsession. We are invited to watch him in his study, to see him in his slippers and jerkin, pen in hand, trying to get his father and uncle off the stairs in fewer than two full chapters, racing to finish his digressions and return to his narrative within the promised time, lowering the curtain on one scene and set of characters in order to open it on another, begging patience and faith, congratulating himself on his occasional triumphs, and wrestling almost everywhere with a thousand problems of time, space, and authorship. The overall comic pleasure, writes Wayne Booth, "the only element which sustains all the disparate elements and combines the other central interests—comic events, comic characters—into any kind of a single whole, is the nature of this action by Tristram: the writing of his book. The work is thus in one sense the dramatized story of a man writing a book."[14]

Sterne's novel is not only "about" the mind of its author. To a considerable extent, like *The Counterfeiters, Remembrance of Things Past*, and *Point Counter Point* (and, like them, musical largely for this reason), it is about that mind in creative motion, the mind as it relates to the problem of autobiography, an insuperable one as he conceives it. And here the identity of form and content is more complete and more evident still. For if *Tristram Shandy* is about the insurmountability of the autobiographical task, given the author's mind and his peculiar conception of his obligation, then what is the form of the novel if not the product and mobile image of that very problem?

*Tristram Shandy*, then, is about the way it is told. Form and content are one and both are process. The moving force in Sterne's novel, as in music and in the musical novel generally, is movement itself. "I cannot write," Sterne complained to David Garrick; "I do a thousand things which cut no figure, *but in the doing.*" The remark, as Denis Donoghue observed, might almost serve as a motto for the entire book. What matters is *how* things are done (or not done—it is all the same). Tristram cuts a figure only in the doing. What holds his attention and ours are the processes of his mind—the associations of his ideas, the gradual shifts and erratic leaps of mind, geography, and mood, the playful manipulation of word and thing—and the problematic procedures of authorship: the author playing, struggling with, and ultimately conquering convention. Northrop Frye was right: "the sense of literature as process was brought to a peculiarly exquisite perfection by Sterne."[15] And the sense of literature as process, of the whole consort of form and content dancing together and blurred to a single figure in dazzling motion, is at least one important sense, source, and purpose of the musicalization of fiction.

Music, as Monroe Beardsley suggests, "is no symbol of time or process, mental or physical, Newtonian or Bergsonian; it *is* process. And perhaps we can say it is the closest thing to pure process, to happening as such, to change abstracted from anything that changes." The great music theorist Heinrich Schenker regarded the musical composition as a complex kinetic organism, and Ernst Kurth agreed with Schenker that "all musical phenomena rest upon kinetic processes and their inner dynamics." For composer Roger Sessions, "the basic ingredient of music is not so much sound as movement," while for psychologist Erwin Straus, "the unity of music and motion is primordial, not artificial, not contrived, and not learned."[16] In short, of all the arts, music is preeminently *the* art of process and motion and the art in which, for that very reason, form and content are inseparable and indistinguishable.

The question of form and content in music has kept composers, musicologists, and philosophers busy at least as far back as Pythagoras, probably, like most such irresolvable disputes, a good deal busier than it should have. I shall make no attempt to resolve the controversy here—that would be almost as presumptuous as futile—but I will try to set down a few of the basic terms of the argument, those relevant to the business at hand. It is well to begin with the explanation that when theorists like Pater, Hanslick, Pratt, and Langer speak of music as pure form or of the fusion of form and content they most often regard *form* not as synonymous with *mould, matrix,* or *pictorial design*—not as fixed shape —but dynamically, as shape developing, shape in the act of unfolding itself. One can, of course, speak of seemingly fixed forms like fugue, rondo, or canon and offer a diagrammatic model of their "form." But that is to miss two important points: first, that these forms are fixed only in their broadest outlines, that they are all more accurately described as rule-governed procedures under varying degrees of governance; second, that the fixed view of form in music (or literature, for that matter) is a violation of the temporality of the art and of our own experience of it. In the sense in which ABA (or first-movement or sonata) form may be viewed in terms of spatial blocks (exposition-development-recapitulation), musical form is of course not at all identical with its content, whatever one's view of the content factor in music. Form in other words is not a detachable framework but, in Pater's words, the distinctive "mode of handling" the subject and materials. In literature, as Thomas Munro observes, "The form must . . . be sought chiefly in the way the expressive materials are organized; the way various associated ideas and images are called up in order—certain beliefs and desires conflicting, events moving toward a climax, or merely dragging along in a slow monotony that itself gives a definite cumulative effect."[17] In the more important and relevant sense, form is not so much shape as "taking shape."

The position one takes on the question of the separability, merger, or identity of form and content in music is likely to depend on whether he regards it as a primarily autonomous or heteronomous art. To the autonomist (or absolutist), the meaning of music is intramusical. It lies wholly within the borders of sound, tone, and motion, and serves neither as a sign, an expression, a symbol, an imitation, a language, nor a likeness of anything other than itself.[18] It has, in other words, no content beyond its own internal formal relationships.

For Eduard Hanslick, the best-known proponent of this formalist-absolutist position, form and content are indistinguishable in music for the quite simple reason that music has no content, no subject, if by subject one means something other than the notes and combinations of notes themselves, that is, form. The analogues with the external world are, for Hanslick, largely subjective impositions. "Now in music, substance and form, the subject and its working out, the image and the realized conception, are mysteriously blended in one undecomposable whole. This complete fusion of substance and form is exclusively characteristic of music, and presents a sharp contrast to poetry, painting, and sculpture, inasmuch as these arts are capable of representing the same idea and the same event in different forms."[19] "Moving patterns of sound," then, are at once the form and content of music.

At the other end of the spectrum are the mimetic-referentialists for whom music is an imitation or representation of a world beyond itself, a world of concepts, creatures, ideas, and events communicated through the music, but not identical with it. In this view music does indeed have a content, one that ranges from the birds and storms often discovered in Beethoven's *Pastorale* symphony and a hundred lesser pieces, through the Fall of Adam in the "falling seventh" chord, to cosmic and psychic harmony. And while the content of music, referentially construed, need not by definition be separate from form, it may be and often is.

There is a substantial body of opinion between these two extremes, most of it fitting somewhere under the heading of expressionism, most of it affirming the existence of some kind of musical content, and most of it nevertheless a good deal closer to Hanslick than to strict mimetic referentialism. Susanne Langer, for example, rejects Hanslick's position as an evasion and yet admits that in its highest attainments, music "exhibits pure form not as an embellishment, but as its very essence." Music does have content, though, and its content, in Langer's view, is human feeling. Music is the "logical expression" of affects and is in a symbolic sense "about them." Even here, form and content, subject and shape, come together through motion, for what music is about and gives unique expression to is the form and moving shape of emotion. "Musical structures logically resemble certain dynamic patterns of human experience."[20] One dynamic pattern resembles and expresses another. The content of music is not musical form, but the form of something else—emotion and the inner life—that can be expressed in no other way and that has precisely the same dynamic and shape. Musical form, in this view, is not identical with content, but is its symbolic representation—if anything a still more accurate description of the peculiar condition of *Tristram Shandy*.

Sterne's contemporaries—theorists like Charles Avison, James Beattie, and Daniel Webb—held positions that were less sophisticated variants of Langer's. Almost all were expressionists, which is to say that they believed strongly in the power of music to mirror and express human feeling. But they, too, put primary and defining emphasis on motion and form and had little patience for trivially imitative content. "Music is imitative," wrote Beattie, "when it readily puts one in mind of the thing imitated. . . . If an explanation be necessary, and if, after all, we find it difficult to recognize any exact similitude I would not call such music an imitation of nature. . . . [Unlike painting] music may be exactly imitative, and yet intolerably bad; or not at all imitative, and yet perfectly good."[21] And if Beattie subordinated imitation to expression, Avison (whom Sterne mentions in *Tristram Shandy*) subordinated expression to the internal demands of the music itself. "Musical expression arises from a Combination of the other two [air and harmony]; and is no other than a strong and proper Application of them to the intended Subject. . . . Air and Harmony, are never to be deserted for the Sake of Expression: Because Expression is founded on them."[22] For Avison, too, the content of the music (its expression) is inseparable from its form (melody and harmony). The composer and music historian Johann Forkel put the case succinctly: "Every musical expression should be brought about by the inner force of art, by the élan of the ideas, and not by aping external graphic occurrences."[23] Sterne would have agreed. The evidence of his own writing suggests that he was an expressionist with a strong autonomist bias. For Sterne, music (and literature as well) was emotively expressive, even imitative of human feeling and thought, yet ultimately a self-contained art. Music could excite the passions, even imitate their sounds, yet finally it maintained its autonomy. Not the discords or the harmonies, but the transitions and relationships between them are what matter; not how high or how low you take it, but being in tune with yourself. There is content in music as there certainly is in *Tristram Shandy*, but in both, content is embodied and absorbed in form and both are dynamic process.

What this points to, and what is in fact true, is that *Tristram Shandy* is, in large and important measure, formalist art.

Because it constructs its own realities—whether using existing materials (including other art works), simulating the "real" world, or employing free invention—formalist art must convince primarily in terms of what takes place within the work of art itself. It is not, as with traditionalist art, primarily accuracy of representation, plausibility of plot, power of psychological insight, depth of feeling, or righteousness of moral doctrine that persuades and convinces. Rather, it is elegance of design and ingenuity of process, precision of rhetoric and adroitness of language, refinement of conceit and nuance of probability, or some combination of these, that enforces belief in and validates formalist art.[24]

*Elegance* is not the word I would use for the design of *Tristram Shandy*, but otherwise this definition will do very well. In its light, Sterne's novel shows up for the weightily if not purely formalist piece it is.

One of the ways it approaches formalism is by taking our attention away from content and fixing it on process. The procedure of the novel makes any normal involvement with plot virtually impossible. After the first few dozen pages or so only a masochist or a critic would try to keep careful track of what is going on—of precisely how old Tristram is at any given time, if indeed he has been born at all; of whether the midwife or Dr. Slop will deliver him when he finally arrives; of whatever became of Trim's poor brother Tom or the more fortunate but still more diligently ignored King of Bohemia. And only a fool would imagine that Tristram's autobiography will ever be completed. So much for the life of Tristram Shandy, Gentleman. The opinions fare a little better. We do manage to find out what Tristram thinks about animal spirits and homunculi, about association and hobbyhorses. But how much more, if this much, do we remember? The opinions that do remain with us are for the most part his opinions about the writing of his book —not merely about how it does not get written, but about how it does—for these are what interest Tristram, and what, by default, he all but compels us to attend to. But there is more than mere opinions at work—these are but a minor part of the game—and more than the fact that any other concentrated investment of interest and expectation is frustrated. There is the endless expectation and frustration itself—not the fact of it, but the feel of it, and ultimately the effect.

The emphasis in *Tristram Shandy*, at every level from

phrase and sentence to chapter, volume, and tale, is on anticipation, postponement, diversion, and frustration; not on
what is provided but on what is not, and still more on the
not providing, at least not when you expected it. Everything
is a kind of riddle. "We live in a world beset on all sides with
mysteries and riddles," observes Tristram; and again content
melts into process, for the ultimate riddle is the "progress"
of the book itself. Here almost everything is a riddle, its
referent, content, meaning, and import unclear and in need
of explanation, clarification, and resolution. The book, like
a complex piece of music, is generated in such a way as to
postpone this awaited clarification, to delay this sense of
resolution and ease for varying, often for unusually and
frustratingly long periods of time. Like a skillful composer
or improviser, Tristram repeatedly generates tension, a
sense of dis-ease, of dissonance—and this not merely at the
level of plot as in any decent mystery or adventure story,
but at every level from the most elemental to the most inclusive. Sentences begin with referents to nonexistent ante-
cedents; and the referents may not be supplied, if they ever
are, until the following sentence or paragraph or until the
end of a long diversionary digression. Sentences end with a
dash, in midair, with their conclusions as uncertain as their
beginnings. Chapters begin in midsentence, events in medias
res with cause, motive, and context unclear and awaiting
revelation. Promises are made and sometimes kept. Some
are cancelled, some merely left dangling (or is that us?),
and so it goes. In short, anticipation is stimulated everywhere and in a hundred ways—in everything from whom
a pronoun may refer to or how a sentence will end to the
oft-promised and nearly undelivered amours of uncle Toby

and the life of Tristram himself, begun ab ovo on page one and ended five years before his birth. The result is to make anticipation and tension themselves rather than their objects the core of the work.

"What a musical stimulus or a series of stimuli indicate and point to are not extramusical concepts and objects but other musical events which are about to happen. That is, one musical event (be it a tone, a phrase, or a whole section) has meaning because it points to and makes us expect another musical event. . . . Embodied [i.e., nonreferential] musical meaning is, in short, a product of expectation"; and "affect or emotion-felt is aroused when an expectation—a tendency to respond—activated by the musical stimulus situation, is temporarily inhibited or permanently blocked."[25] In music, then, nondesignative meaning—and it is the principal kind—derives not from external reference but from the arousal of internal expectation, and emotion is the product not primarily of what is provided (in literature the thing described) but of the blocking of that expectation (the experience of *not* immediately receiving the expected object or description). Emotion and meaning in music, viewed from an absolutist perspective, are functions of expectation and frustration, and it should be clear to any reader of *Tristram Shandy* that while there are undeniably other sources of both in the novel, it relies for its effects far more extensively and pervasively on the creation of anticipation and the inhibition of response at every level and at almost every moment than traditional fiction does.

*Tristram Shandy*, in other words, is an enclosed system of tensions and releases, of resolutions (or nonresolutions) of discords and harmonies; and as Tristram tells us, it is the

"how" that matters. After a while the reader begins to ac-
climate to the repeated violations of literary convention and
watches them evolve into a kind of free-wheeling convention of their own. He does not lose sight of where he is
headed or what he has been promised—that would spoil the
game—but he is at least as interested in how he will be pre-
vented from arriving or how he will finally arrive as he is in
the arrival itself, and often more affected by the arrival *as
arrival*, as a resolution of tension, than as an object of description or discourse. Meaning, too—partly in the contex-
tual, partly in the designative sense—is, like nondesignative
meaning in music, largely a matter of the stimulation of
expectancy and the delay or frustration of fulfillment. In
one sense, the import of many of the digressions and of much
of the plot they digress from is more properly understood
in terms of preparation, departure, delay, and return than
in terms of whatever referential significance they may intrinsically have. But meaning grows out of expectancy and
frustration in another, broader, more designative sense: it
is part of the moving picture of the author's mind. Process
is meaning. The shape of the novel as a labyrinthine pattern
of anticipation, postponement, and resolution is at the same
time the shape of the mind that is the subject of the novel—
the eccentric mind of Tristram Shandy in creative motion.

"*All art*," reads Pater's famous dictum, "*constantly aspires toward the condition of music.*" While Pater's claim
is far too sweeping and a far more accurate account of the
aesthetic impulses of his own time than of art generally, it
offers us pertinent insight into the nature and achievement
of *Tristram Shandy*. Quite unmistakably and whatever its
aspirations, Sterne's exotic and prevenient novel rises to

the condition of music as Pater defines it, achieving, or very nearly, what all art presumably aspires to:

For while in all other kinds of art it is possible to distinguish the matter from the form, and the understanding can always make this distinction, yet it is the constant effort of art to obliterate it. That the mere matter of a poem, for instance, its subject, namely, its given incidents or situation—that the mere matter of a picture, the actual circumstances of an event, the actual topography of a landscape—should be nothing without the form, the spirit, of the handling, that this form, this mode of handling, should become an end in itself, should penetrate every part of the matter: this is what all art constantly strives after, and achieves in different degrees. . . .

Art, then, is thus always striving to be independent of the mere intelligence, to become a matter of pure perception, to get rid of its responsibilities to its subject or material; the ideal examples of poetry and painting being those in which the constituent elements of the composition are so welded together, that the material or subject no longer strikes the intellect only; nor the form, the eye or the ear only; but form and matter, in their union or identity, present one single effect to the "imaginative reason," that complex faculty for which every thought and feeling is twinborn with its sensible analogue or symbol.

It is the art of music which most completely realizes this artistic ideal, this perfect identification of matter and form. In its consummate moments, the end is not distinct from the means, the form from the matter, the subject from the expression; they inhere in and completely saturate each other; and to it, therefore, to the condition of its perfect moments, all the arts may be supposed constantly to tend and aspire. In music, then, rather than in poetry, is to be found the true type or measure of perfected art. Therefore, although each art has its incommunicable element, its untranslatable order of impressions, its unique mode of reaching the "imaginative reason," yet the arts may be represented as continually struggling after the law or principle of music, to a condition which music alone completely realises.[26]

## Improvisation

The fact that Sterne was at least a reasonably proficient viola da gambist is important for what it implies about Sterne's general familiarity with music. But it also has a more specific relevance to certain characteristics of *Tristram Shandy.* The bass viol (or viola da gamba), whose natural function was to play a bass part,

was much used for improvisation, the favourite form being the varying of a short bass theme, possibly taken from a song- or dance-melody. It had also adopted from the lute the practice of playing chords and presenting the semblance of polyphony, and this enabled it to combine melody and accompaniment in the most ingenious and suggestive manner. In England the bass viol was still cultivated at a time when the violin was triumphing everywhere else. . . . The bass-viol style of playing formed the foundation of the violin sonata, which inherited from it the partiality for embroidering a bass with brilliant runs, arpeggios, and other embellishments. From the bass viol the violin also acquired its love of variation, as well as its readiness to abandon the continuo and build up a polyphonic structure out of its own resources. The tradition of this style was preserved for many years in the German violin sonata. We owe to it the marvels of Bach's unaccompanied sonatas and partitas.[27]

This account of bass viol performance, with its characteristic emphasis on virtuoso improvisation, embellishment, variation, and polyphonic invention, reads like a compendium of Shandean procedures, and it takes us back to the other side of Tristram's authorial Janus, that of the vagarious, spontaneous composer, the man who begins "with writing the first sentence——and trusting to Almighty God for the second" (8:2.540). Just as the opposite face of Tristram-as-author primps itself in the mirror of internal harmony and perpetual motion, this finds its image in the improvisatory style of late baroque music.

Free forms such as the prelude—a generic name for any composition without a specific formal structure—fantasy, elegy, impromptu, and capriccio were among the most popular musical forms in Sterne's time. The extemporaneous style from which they evolved was a roccoco or late baroque development evident in some of the works of J. S. Bach, Mattheson, and Telemann, but reaching its height during the years 1740–1780. The essence of the new "style galant" was liberation from the rules that the new composers, theorists, and performers felt had restricted their predecessors. This was the age of improvisation and ornamentation, the age of virtuosity—in instrumental performance no less than in the famous abuses of the Italian primadonnas. Virtuoso performers of the eighteenth century typically "regarded the composer's own text as a challenge to their inventiveness and resource, a basic canvas to be embellished here and there with variations, roulades and divisions. . . . The performer could legitimately feel that it was not only his right but also his duty to make a substantial creative contribution of his own to the music he was performing." The style was marked by elaborate ornamentation—glittering sequences of trills, turns, springers, and slides—by rapid divisions improvised over a persistent bass, by pyrotechnical cadenzas where the performer extemporized elaborate fantasies on the principal themes of the movement, and on occasion by the spontaneous improvisation of an entire movement or a complete fugue (as in some of Handel's organ concertos). "Any picture of this music," as Thurston Dart insists, "will be impossibly distorted unless and until it is realized how big was the part that extemporization played."[28]

The new style found its fullest expression in Italy; Handel, England's leading composer during Sterne's adult life and a man whose domination of English music was all but total, was steeped in the Italian tradition. Handel's standard practice was to provide only a basic outline of the music in his notation, leaving ample room for elaborate improvisational play. His organ concertos, "interpolated in his oratorios, were universally admired for their wonderful polyphonic elaboration, yet the printed scores seem almost insignificant and certainly do not give the remotest idea of how they were played." An organist performing a chorale prelude, for example, was expected to parade his improvisational powers in full dress, and themes were often obscured behind a dazzling procession of free elaborations and embellishments. The clavier pieces, most characteristic of the period, were buried under waves of grace notes and embellishments, so that it is often virtually impossible to follow the continuity of the original melody.[29]

All this was to the performer's credit, for late baroque theorists and audiences shared the composer's conviction that embellishments were an essential part of the music and indispensable to it. In his treatise on the art of clavier playing (1753), Carl Philipp Emanuel Bach observed that

No one, perhaps, has ever questioned the necessity of embellishments. We may perceive this from our meeting them everywhere in great abundance. Indeed, when we consider the good they do they are indispensable. They tie the notes together; they enliven them; they give them, when necessary, a special emphasis and weight; they make them pleasing and hence arouse a special attention; they help to clarify their content; whatever its nature, whether sad, gay, or any other sort we please, they invariably contribute their share.[30]

C.P.E. Bach's music has itself been described as "full of sighs, echoes, and tearful effusions, yet in the quick movements also full of surprises and unconventional, not to say coquettish, details";[31] the description might be transferred, virtually unchanged, to *Tristram Shandy*. For Bach, the ornaments were "necessary," even "indispensable," and they contributed their share. But others were willing to take embellishment further still, to make it the first order of musical business. Embellishments are "greatly befitted to move powerfully the soul; to deprive music of such ornaments would be depriving it of the most beautiful part of its essence."[32] Essentially, this is Tristram's attitude as well. To him the digressions, the embellishments and elaborations of his basic story, are incontestably "the sunshine" of the work. They are "the life, the soul of reading;——take them out of this book for instance,——you might as well take the book along with them;——one cold eternal winter would reign in every page of it; restore them to the writer;——he steps forth like a bridegroom,——bids All hail; brings in variety, and forbids the appetite to fail" (1:22. 73).

In his improvising posture Tristram insists that vagary is his only master, that he follows "no man's rules who ever lived." If the boast were valid the analogy would suffer, for while improvisation often created an illusion of complete freedom (in the fantasia, for example), it was governed by an ample body of rules and conventions. In point of fact, however, Tristram's claim, while occasionally justified, ultimately collapses under a careful reading of his book. Even if Tristram took his contention seriously, Laurence Sterne knew better; and more important, the rules and procedures that guided him—elaborate digression via the association of ideas and impulses, the principle of internal balance and harmony, the maintenance of at least a minimally recognizable framework around which the embellish-

ments take place, "dividing the ground," the sudden and
surprising return—all are among the principal conventions and procedures that guided the art of musical improvisation. As with the eighteenth-century "free forms," in
other words, the apparent anarchy of *Tristram Shandy* is
for the most part only apparent, and Raguenet's description
of the typical eighteenth-century Italian virtuoso is equally
applicable to the pyrotechnical deceptions of our narrator:

He'll have passages of such an extent as will perfectly confound
his auditors at first, and upon such irregular notes as shall instill a
terror as well as surprise into the audience, who will immediately
conclude that the whole concert is degenerating into a dreadful
dissonance; and betraying 'em by that means into a concern for
the music, which seems to be on the brink of ruin, he immediately
reconciles 'em by such regular cadences that everyone is surprised
to see harmony rising again, in a manner, out of discord itself and
owing its greatest beauties to those irregularities which seemed to
threaten it with destruction.[33]

Viewed from this angle, Tristram's contradictory pos-
tures are surprisingly complementary, for in a sense it is
the improvisatory character of the novel, its seeming un-
accountability and lack of control, that accounts for its singular fusion of form and content and justifies Tristram's
claim to governance. When Tristram finally emerges out of
the maddening chaos of his narration, it becomes clear that
process has been content, chaos order, and madness meaning. The business of the novel is self-revelation in the often
impetuous and improvisatory act of revealing itself. Its
aim is to show us fitful mind and erratic character by letting
the presenting mind behave fitfully and erratically; in such
an enterprise the at least apparent absence of control is the
very proof of its presence. The important element of truth
in the first stance—that Tristram does to a considerable

extent pursue his impulses—engenders the element of truth in his seemingly contradictory claim that he does in fact know what he is about, for what he is about, as we have said, is in large part the presentation of the impulsive nature of mind and the consequences of that nature for the once quite steady business of autobiography.

---

## *Music and the Inner Life*

There is musicality in the identity of form and content, in the primacy of motion and process, and in the improvisatory techniques. But to understand fully the role of music in *Tristram Shandy*, one must look to the common element in all three—the nature of thought, feeling, and the inner life. A letter will help clarify the connection:

A long, sentimental reminiscence of my childhood! Yes, I actually believed for a moment that by some such circumferential snare as that I might trap you, bring you within my range, sting, and poison you with the subtle-sweet poison of a shared experience and consciousness. That again is highly characteristic of me. It is precisely the sort of thing I am always trying to do in my writing—to present my unhappy reader with a wide-ranged chaos—of actions and reactions, thoughts, memories and feelings—in the vain hope that at the end he will see that the whole thing represents only *one moment, one feeling, one person*. A raging, trumpeting jungle of associations, and then I announce at the end of it, with a gesture of despair, "This is I!" [34]

No, the letter was not written by either Tristram or Sterne. It was written by Demarest, the autobiographical hero of Conrad Aiken's novel, *Blue Voyage*. And it is a letter that describes not only the authorial intentions of Demarest, but more important of Aiken himself, a writer whose poetry and fiction, perhaps more than that of any other author of our time, aspires to the mood, form, effects, and "condition" of music.

Aiken is candid and articulate about his musical intentions, confessing to "some complex which has always given me a strong bias towards an architectural structure in poetry analogous to that of music." Sterne's metaphors and practice testify to a similar bias, and they rise from a similar source.

Once Sterne turned away from a duration plot and from simply crystallized character, he was faced with the greatest problem of all—the problem of an ultimate form which could be raised from the material quite naturally seen and felt, a form which should derive no curve or mass from the selective magnetic force of preconceptions of action and of character. A hundred and seventy-five years later, novelists are still seeking solutions for these problems which he first confronted.[35]

Sterne's "solution," if such it may be called—such problems are not solved, they are only bargained with—was to bring to the novel what Aiken brought to his poetry and fiction, "an architectural structure analogous to that of music." Why?

Demarest's letter suggests two answers. The first is consciousness. Like Sterne, Aiken is less interested in the interrelationships between man and man or between man and his social or physical surroundings than he is, as the letter suggests, in what takes place inside us: in the nature and simultaneous complexities of thought and feeling, the problems of personal wholeness, identity, and self-presentation. Aiken and Sterne are concerned with interiority, with the forms of mental and emotional experience, their architecture as it were, and with the special qualities and effects of that experience. Music is pertinent here in two ways. First, consciousness is amorphous stuff, and mythology is not alone in identifying ooze with chaos. To write about consciousness, to make the pour of thought the foundation of a work of literature, is to risk what literature cannot bear too much of—utter formlessness. Music is a fertile source of rational structure, and writers like Joyce, Proust, and Aiken, among others, have used music as an instrument of structure and control, giving shape to the mental flow. Music, in other words, may have served Sterne simply as scaffolding to hold his gingerbread castle of the mind together, as a structural frame over and around which his improvisational fancy (his own rendering of consciousness) could be given free rein without the risk of total chaos.

But music is more than a mere scaffolding for the mind; it is also an analogue of it. In the expressionist view, music's hold over us takes much of its strength from the relationship between musical patterns and processes and the inner life of man. The identification of music with the psychic life is a commonplace. Wolfgang Köhler, one of the founders of Gestalt psychology, remarks that "Quite generally, the inner processes, whether emotional or intellectual, show types of development which may be given names, usually applied to musical events, such as: *crescendo* and *diminuendo, accelerando* and *ritardando.*"[36] Aiken reveals his own identification with this position in an extended simile:

> Things mused upon are, in the mind, like music,
> They flow, they have a rhythm, they close and open,
> And sweetly return upon themselves in rhyme.
> Against the darkness they are woven,
> They are lost for a little, and laugh again,
> They fall or climb.[37]

For Hegel, music's principal task is "echoing the motions of the inmost self." Bergson, whose concept of psychological time is remarkably close to Sterne's, defines personality as the "uninterrupted melody of our interior life"[38] and regards music, the most purely temporal of the arts, as superior to the others because a more faithful image of the fundamental self, of the sense of succession that defines experience. "The upshot of all these speculative researches," concludes Susanne Langer, is that

> there are certain aspects of the so-called "inner life"—physical or mental—which have formal properties similar to those of music— patterns of motion and rest, of tension and release, of agreement and disagreement, preparation, fulfilment, excitation, sudden change, etc.
>
> So the first requirement for a connotative relationship between music and subjective experience, a certain similarity of logical form, is certainly satisfied.[39]

But even without these speculative researches one might have been brought to a similar conclusion. Indeed, there may be no better evidence for the relationship between music and the inner life, the motions of thought and feeling, than literary practice—the fact that authors who attempt to represent this inner life so often render it, wittingly or no, in terms of musical patterns and procedures. That some have deliberately turned to music as an analogue of consciousness may only demonstrate their rational belief in the validity of the analogy. That others may have spontaneously generated musical techniques and structures in the attempt to represent the flow of inner experience is perhaps a more persuasive testimonial to the analogousness of music. "One is often led to suspect," as Melvin Friedman concludes, that the modern novel depends so heavily on borrowings from music because "the only analogy with the important sequence of the unfolding states of consciousness is musical structure or pattern."[40]

Simultaneity, the impingement of past and future on present and vice versa, the interrelationship, repetition, and overlapping of ideas, the intricate and mysterious associations of those ideas, and the sudden or prepared transitions between thoughts, attitudes, and emotions—all are characteristic of the processes of interior experience, all are characteristic of the processes of musical development, all are of singular concern to Conrad Aiken, and all are numbered among the qualities and obsessive themes of *Tristram Shandy*. In his search for an appropriate formal analogue for subjective experience, Sterne—like Proust, Joyce, Gide, Mann, Aiken, and other "composers" of fiction—was drawn almost inevitably to music. The musicality of his novel is inherent in its preoccupations, in its fidelity to the inner life of man.

Demarest's letter also points to a second source of the musicality of *Tristram Shandy*. His effort, he tells us, has been "to present my unhappy reader with a wide-ranged chaos,—of actions and reactions, thoughts, memories, and feelings,—in the vain hope that at the end he will see that the whole thing represents only *one moment, one feeling, one person*." The syntax is too studied, and I would want to qualify that "one moment, one feeling" somewhat, but otherwise the lines might have been Tristram's; they are an accurate description of his own absurd but heroic effort. Tristram too would recreate the conflicting and often contradictory movements of consciousness, of self and world, will and possibility, perception and reality; he would recreate the chaos of thought, memory, action, and feeling; and he would make an aesthetic object of this flood, the realistic artifice of *Tristram Shandy*. Tristram has said that he would follow the rules of no man who ever lived, but he has not said he will follow no rules. He will bring unity out of chaos, if only by making chaos the only unity—we are back to the contrary narrative poses—or, to put it another way, he will resolve discord into harmony; and now we are back to writing as humming and to the concept of the musical novel.

The attempt to harmonize dissonant and discordant contraries is among the chief motives behind the musicalization of fiction. Virginia Woolf spoke of her need to "put everything in; yet to saturate," to include all the stubborn facts of external experience yet unite them in the unity of consciousness, of "the moment." André Gide sought an all-inclusive presentation of self with all its contradictions, dissonances, and distortions, one that would somehow embody these distortions in appropriate forms. For Gide as for Woolf, the appropriate formal analogue is often music, and Wackenroder and Tieck articulate the reason: Music is the only art form which "reduces the most manifold and most contradictory movements of our soul to the *same* beautiful harmonies."[41] In a passage from *Der Kurgast*, Hesse wrote, "If I were a musician I could write without difficulty a melody in two voices. . . . And anyone who can read music, could read my double melody, could see and hear in each tone its counterpoint, the brother, the enemy, the antipode."[42] And Hesse longs to be a musician, as Ralph Freedman points out, "because music embodies the very concept of harmony within dissonance which is his prevailing theme."[43]

Tristram too would be such a musician. He would be the

composer of consciousness, and consciousness is not merely mobile, transient, and elusive; it is also irrational, vacillatory, deceptive, and contradictory. Music can "put everything in," be saturated with dissonance, yet resolve it all in the final harmony, not necessarily of feeling and idea, but of process, design, and personality. In Tristram's hands it can, at any rate, try.

# 3

## Simultaneity, Time, and the Art of Literary Counterpoint

Poor Tristram, hapless victim of a thousand mischances of nature, nurture, the Shandean and the human conditions, is by nothing so mercilessly misused as by time. We are all time's playthings, thrown away when it has done with us, the dying Tristram (and his creator) more than most: "Time wastes too fast: every letter I trace tells me with what rapidity Life follows my pen; the days and hours of it, more precious, my dear *Jenny!* than the rubies about thy neck, are flying over our heads like light clouds of a windy day, never to return more——every thing presses on" (9:8.610–11). But the flight from time's consequences is but one aspect of his problem. The other side—his vain pursuit of the very enemy he flees—is far more complex and troublesome. Tristram's battle is built into his effort. The fact that his is a book written about the writing of a book almost of itself guarantees his entanglement in a network of temporal complexities and pursuits.

Tristram is an author writing in the present about the events of a multiplex past, weighing and responding to obligations and difficulties that press him from the immediate future, and addressing readers in an expanding, indeterminate one. There are, then, three fixed parts in the composition: the author, his characters, and his readers, each of them not only stationed at different points in time—present, past, and future—but, as actors in the complex drama that brings them together, each proceeding at a different pace. There is first of all the time of actual occurrence, the real duration of an event. There is also writing time, the usually much longer time it takes Tristram to write about it. And between the two, moving at its own intermediate pace somewhere in the unknowable future, there is the time it takes Sir or Madame, Tristram's assiduous readers, to read about it. In one sense the three temporal modes are separate and separable, but in another they are neither, for there is one "place" where all three are going on together—in the author's all-inclusive mind. He is sitting at his desk, writing or musing at one tempo about recollected events that moved at another and elbow each other for space, imagining his readers following both sequences at yet a third.

Perhaps most frustrating, because most difficult to reconcile, is the relationship between the time consumed by events in the world and the exponentially greater time it takes to write about them. Tristram, victim of the association of his ideas and a compulsive-digressive need to fill all in, is progressing in his tale at a rate a good deal slower than he lives, three hundred and sixty-four times as slowly to be precise. As a result, the completion of his autobiography is a physical and mathematical impossibility: "In short there is no end of it; ... I have been at it these six weeks, making all the speed I possibly could——and am not yet born" (1:14.37). Worse still, the gap between his obligation and his achievement threatens to multiply itself three hundred and sixty-four times every day, dropping the staggering author farther and farther behind his ever-receding goal.

The pursuit of time and the flight from it are but two

perspectives on the same race. The frantic flight from death in volume 7 is but the obverse of the equally frantic effort throughout the narrative to hold time still, to render it more tractable to Tristram's will and bring the disparate temporal modes into harmonious relation—reader, writer, and actor all abreast and nose to nose at the wire. It will never work, of course, but that only heightens the frustration and concern. The swiftness of time's flow, its evanescence and vexing irretrievability, is one of the obsessive Tristram's most persistent obsessions. It is also the experiential core of musical motion. In its fleeting elusiveness, music is the very image of Tristram's problem, but while they share a common trait, the writer's plague is music's virtue. As Roger Sessions puts it, the "essential and inherent quality of music [is] . . . its fluidity, the fact that it is an art, even the art par excellence, of time. . . . In music each moment is fleeting; it passes and cannot be completely recaptured."[1] This same problem of transience and irretrievability also troubled and fascinated Robert Browning and accounts in large part for his adoption of musical techniques in such poems as the "Parleying" with Charles Avison, "Abt Vogler," "A Tocatta of Galuppi's," and "Master Hughes of Saxe-Gothe." For Browning, music seems to represent almost precisely what it represents for Sterne: the sense of life as a movement seeking resolution, the form in movement of the soul itself rather than the rigid categories of the mind.[2]

*Tristram Shandy* is a hall of mirrors. Nothing is quite separable there, nothing quite distinct. If the flight from time is but the pursuit viewed from the other end of the track, the irretrievability is likewise as much image as substance. It is the partial reflection and consequence of the problem of simultaneity. Once again, to complicate the maze, art is life, life art: Tristram's sense of an uncontrollable, runaway time stems largely from his narrative effort to bring a sense of simultaneity to a linear medium; the mortal problem of fleeting time is in part product of the aesthetic problem of simultaneous presentation.

Tristram is an autobiographer with far more than his own story to tell. There is the story of young Tristram, to be sure, but if we are to understand him—boy and man— we must be acquainted with the causes of his anomalous development, with the people and events who made him the strange erratic creature he is. We must also suffer the consequences of that development. As guests of that same mind we will share the room, like it or not, with whatever else enters it during our stay. What this means is that the story of Tristram Shandy, Gentleman, as that gentleman has prepared it (or let it flow), is a thousand other stories besides. It is also the story of uncle Toby and Trim, their campaigns on the bowling green, of uncle Toby's wound, his "amours" with the Widow Wadman, the death of LeFever, the jailing of Trim's brother, the history and sermons of Yorick, the story of Aunt Dinah, "Slawkenbergius's Tale," and so on to the virtual obliteration of the putative subject itself. Nor is that all. Events are but part of the story. What matters, as Sterne's epigraph indicates, is not events but our opinions about them, so these too must take their place, and prominently. And what about the adult Tristram, the man whose unenviable responsibility it is to relate all these tales and opinions? Ultimately, it turns out, this is *his* book, the story of his life and opinions. More accurately, if somewhat confusingly, it is the story of his mind as the teller of its story; so we are supplied with heavy doses of his own opinions, attitudes, impressions, and perplexities, principally about the writing of his book.

All this would be heavy work for any author, but for Tristram the difficulties are compounded many times over; he has abandoned the convenient but deceptive artifice of narrative linearity in favor of an ultimately unmanageable but unmistakably more appropriate form, a legitimate formal analogue for experience. Tristram diligently if foolhardily persists in the effort to present his world not as the novel, limited to print and page, has traditionally presented it, but in the form truest to objective and subjective reality. Events in the physical world do not mould themselves to the limitations of traditional narrative. They do not occur as the author is obliged to display them, seriatim, but as often simultaneously; and Tristram, who shrinks from no task except perhaps that of going easy on himself and his readers, strives for an accurate empirical account of this complexity. But this is only the first turn in the maze. In a book about its own production, one of the most salient features of "external reality" is the act of literary creation. That events external to himself occur together is only one facet of objective simultaneity; another is their description. Once an action is set in motion it takes on a reality of its own and that reality is likely to be coextensive not only with other events in its own world—the "historical reality" of Walter Shandy's household and the bowling green— but with other events within the larger fictive framework that includes the author as adult narrator. Simultaneity is not only a reality within the lives of Tristram's characters; it is also a function of the author's relation to them.

But the ultimate residence of simultaneity in the novel is

the only real home of everything in it: the mind of Tristram himself. Simultaneity pertains among characters, between character and reader, author and reader, author and character, but ultimately it is all, to state endless perplexity as cliché, in his own mind. What matters is not what "is," whatever that may "be," but what is presented, and what and how the world of the novel is made manifest is strictly a matter of mind. In the final analysis everything exists only there. Reader, character, history, and self are but other names for projection, invention, recollection, and perception. And simultaneous occurrence is a fact of all their lives. The same is true of their temporal modes. The only real time is the dynamic present, which includes past and future as it includes sensations, emotions, and opinions: as dissolving ingredients in the primordial subjective ooze.[3]

Once again Sterne's novel shares common ground with music. According to at least one view, the simultaneity of past, present, and future is integral to the very nature of musical time:

Musical time does not have an objective, abstract, "non-musical" future and past as its orientation. It sets up, so to speak, its own future and past, and it does this *constantly in the process of its own motion.* . . . This is the very essence of musical motion: the constant creation of a future and a past in the actual present moment, in *each* present moment. Even this moment is not present in the strict sense; it is not there in front of the listener in the manner of an object. The moment of musical time is not present, it is at best present*ing*, creating the temporal tension of what has gone before and what is to come, the tension of the whole in the moment.[4]

*Tristram Shandy*, like a musical composition, is all dynamic process, all fluid motion. Time in the novel is a continually unfolding present that cannot be defined or understood independently of where it has come from and where it may be going, that continually sets up its own future and past and includes both within it as memory and projection. It is mind we are observing, and memory and anticipation are no less components of mind than present perception. They influence and are in turn altered by the present they intrude on. Shandean motion is musical motion. It is never quite *there*, never a static or measurable unit. It is always fleeting, always becoming, and past and future, often together, are integral parts of that becoming. "A cow broke in (tomorrow morning) to my uncle Toby's fortifications." "The door opens in the next chapter but one." Where are we? In the book or in the world? In the past with the cow and the door, in the future with "tomorrow morning" and the chapter after next, or in the present with the literary harlequin who juggles them all on stage, who is, as Joan Stambaugh puts it, "present*ing*, creating the temporal tension of what has gone before and what is to come, the tension of the whole in the moment." These are tours de force, the fetes that bring the house down, but the juggler is always on stage, the clubs always in the air.

Past, present, and future; character, author, and reader; recollection, perception, and reflection; event, emotion, and idea—these are the circus animals of Tristram's mind, and they are always on call. Tristram would give us what conventional novelists have shied away from—a true picture of human experience in all its stubbornness and complexity, and to do so he must confront directly, as conventional fiction did not, the problem of simultaneity. It is a problem only music handles with ease—through harmony, through temporal absorption in the all-inclusive present, but perhaps most important for Tristram, through counterpoint.

The problem of simultaneity in literature is in principle insuperable. Try as he may, the writer, unlike the composer, can present his audience with only one thing at a time. The textural density of actual experience must be decomposed and laid out in a linear sequence that conforms to the topographical limitations of the art but violates the experience art would reproduce. A number of recent authors—including Gide, Joyce, Aiken, and Huxley, and Flaubert and DeQuincey before them—faced or merely infatuated with this irrevocable limitation of their medium, have tried in various ways and with varying degrees of success to overcome it. Most often, as in much of Aiken's verse, in the sirens section of *Ulysses*, and in Huxley's *Point Counter Point*, for example, the attempt takes the form of a rapid alternation between contrasting tones, themes, emotions, dialogue, or events. The goal is to imply, through the rapidity and contrast of the juxtaposition, through a technique of interruption and overlap, or through more overt designation, that the events we are witnessing are occurring together and to simulate, within the limitations of a linear medium, the effects of counterpoint. Some two centuries earlier, similarly concerned with multiple consciousness and simultaneous occurrence and the problems of representation they raise, Sterne laid the foundation for future sophistication of the technique and took it as far as most of his successors, Joyce and a very few others excepted.

Not all simultaneity is musical and not all musical simultaneity is counterpoint. Much of what happens in *Tristram Shandy*, however, is both. The rapid oscillation between contrasting words, themes, situations, characters, and utterances is everywhere in the novel; many of these elements are temporally co-present in the external world or in Tris-

tram's mind, if not on the printed page, and many of them
are conspicuously, even overtly, musical. The ingenious
treatment of the whiskers affair is a striking example. Tristram begins it with a statement of his theme, centering
"Upon Whiskers" on the page, interrupts himself to introduce a "Fragment" illustrative of how that theme may
be expanded, and is off, throwing it back and forth between several rapidly alternating voices:

> You are half asleep, my good lady, said the old gentleman, taking
> hold of the old lady's hand, and giving it a gentle squeeze, as he
> pronounced the word *Whiskers*——shall we change the subject?
> By no means, replied the old lady. . . .
>     The old gentleman went on as follows.——Whiskers! cried
> the queen of *Navarre*, dropping her knotting-ball as *La Fosseuse*
> uttered the word—Whiskers; madam, said *La Fosseuse*, pinning the
> ball to the queen's apron, and making a courtesy as she repeated it.

At this point the distinctive tone and dynamics of the various voices are emphasized: "*La Fosseuse*'s voice was naturally soft and low, yet 'twas an articulate voice: and every
letter of the word *whiskers* fell distinctly upon the queen
of *Navarre*'s ear——Whiskers! cried the queen, laying a
greater stress upon the word, and as if she had still distrusted
her ears——Whiskers; replied *La Fosseuse*, repeating the
word a third time." Here the theme is given a historical elaboration describing its discreet and indiscreet uses
throughout the kingdom and its application to both gal-
lantry and devotion. A new motive is then introdced in
the figure of the handsome but whiskerless young Sieur *de
Croix*, and a new voice in the person of the lady De Baussiere who fell in love with him: "But he has no whiskers,
cried *La Fosseuse*——Not a pile, said *La Rebours*." And
now the theme is more elaborately embellished in a number
of voices, each displaying its special virtuosity:

The queen went directly to her oratory, musing all the way, as she walked through the gallery, upon the subject; turning it this way and that way in her fancy. . . .

La Guyol, La Battarelle, La Maronette, La Sabatiere, retired instantly to their chambers——Whiskers! said all four of them to themselves, as they bolted their doors on the inside.

The Lady Carnavallette embellishes the theme with divisions, breaking it into smaller parts, the Lady Baussiere virtually losing her way in an even more glittering display of ornamental virtuosity:

The Lady *Carnavallette* was counting her beads with both hands, unsuspected under her farthingal——from St. *Antony* down to St. *Ursula* inclusive, not a saint passed through her fingers without whiskers; St. *Francis*, St. *Dominick*, St. *Bennet*, St. *Basil*, St. *Bridget*, had all whiskers.

The Lady *Baussiere* had got into a wilderness of conceits, with moralizing too intricately upon *La Fosseuse*'s text——She mounted her palfry, her page followed her——the host passed by.

The fireworks have gone far enough now and the virtuoso, seeking refuge in repetition, drops Lady Baussiere's theme into a basso ostinato sounded, sustained and going its unperturbed way beneath a new melody weaving threateningly above it:

The Lady *Baussiere* rode on.

One denier, cried the order of mercy——one single denier in behalf of a thousand patient captives, whose eyes look towards heaven and you for their redemption.

——The Lady *Baussiere* rode on.

Pity the unhappy, said a devout, venerable, hoary-headed man, meekly holding up a box, begirt with iron, in his withered hands ——I beg for the unfortunate——good, my Lady, 'tis for a prison ——for an hospital——'tis for an old man——a poor man undone by shipwreck, by suretyship, by fire——I call God and all his angels to witness——'tis to cloath the naked——to feed the hungry——'tis to comfort the sick and the broken hearted.

The Lady *Baussiere* rode on.

A decayed kinsman bowed himself to the ground.

——The Lady *Baussiere* rode on.

He ran begging bare-headed on one side of her palfry, conjuring her by the former bonds of friendship, alliance, consanguinity, &c.——Cousin, aunt, sister, mother——for virtue's sake, for your own, for mine, for Christ's sake remember me——pity me.

——The Lady *Baussiere* rode on.

Take hold of my whiskers, said the Lady *Baussiere*——The page took hold of her palfry. She dismounted at the end of the terrace. (5:1.343-46)

A still more extraordinary exploitation of contrapuntal technique is the troping of Trim's reading of Yorick's sermon on conscience. The sermon is four-voice counterpoint, Trim reading the basic text to the periodic and increasingly prominent and obscuring accompaniment of bracketed commentary—first by Dr. Slop and Walter, later by uncle Toby, and by Trim himself. Trim reads, Slop comments. Trim continues, apparently undisturbed and uninterrupted, and Slop interposes a more defiant claim. Trim goes on, and Walter compliments his reading. Trim, carrying the principal theme of the piece in the bass voice, perseveres beneath the plaudits and complaints, only to find them multiplying above him as the two upper voices enter into a counterpointed duel and are joined by a fourth voice, uncle Toby.

"that it is not a matter of *trust*, as the Apostle intimates,——but a matter of *certainty* and fact, that the conscience is good, and that the man must be good also."

[Then the Apostle is altogether in the wrong, I suppose, quoth Dr. *Slop*, and the Protestant divine is in the right. Sir, have patience, replied my father, for I think it will presently appear that *St. Paul* and the Protestant divine are both of an opinion.——As nearly so, quoth Dr. *Slop*, as east is to west;——but this, continued he, lifting both hands, comes from the liberty of the press.

It is no more, at the worst, replied my uncle *Toby*, than the liberty of the pulpit; for it does not appear that the sermon is printed, or ever likely to be.

Go on, *Trim,* quoth my father.] (2:17.126–27)

Trim goes on, but the piece is complicated further by the increased and provocative participation of the fourth voice. Toby engages Slop with a pregnant "Humph! . . . not accented as a note of acquiescence," and "Dr. *Slop,* who had an ear, understood my uncle *Toby* as well as if he had wrote a whole volume against the seven sacraments.——Humph! replied Dr. *Slop,* (stating my uncle *Toby*'s argument over again to him)" (2:17.129), and he is off on a series of brief variations on the number seven.

Trim recovers himself for the moment and brings back the principal theme, the sermon itself, but he cannot stave off the forces of polyphonic invention and embellishment for long. Toward the end, his own impassioned responses and interpolations overwhelm him. He yields up the melody to Walter (the third voice) and takes on the role of accompanist:

"Observe the last movement of that horrid engine!" [I would rather face a cannon, quoth *Trim,* stamping.]——"See what convulsions it has thrown him into!——Consider the nature of the posture in which he now lies stretched ——what exquisite tortures he endures by it!"——[I hope 'tis not in *Portugal.*]——" 'Tis all nature can bear! Good God! see how it keeps his weary soul hanging upon his trembling lips!" [I would not read another line of it, quoth *Trim,* for all this world;——I fear, an' please your Honours, all this is in *Portugal,* where my poor brother *Tom* is. I tell thee *Trim,* again, quoth my father, 'tis not an historical account,——'tis a description.——'Tis only a description, honest man, quoth *Slop,* there's not a word of truth in it.——That's another story, replied my father.——However, as *Trim* reads it with so much concern, ——'tis cruelty to force him to go on with it.——Give me hold of the sermon, *Trim,* ——I'll finish it for thee, and thou mayst go. I must stay and hear it too, replied *Trim,* if your Honour will allow

me;——tho' I would not read it myself for a Colonel's pay.——
Poor *Trim*! quoth my uncle *Toby*. My father went on.] (2:17.139)

This rapid alternation and juxtaposition for contrapuntal
effect may certainly be viewed as an imperfect imitation of
musical counterpoint, the illusion of simultaneity masking
as simultaneity. It may also be read as a quite comfortable
literary adaptation and counterpart of an actual contrapuntal procedure mastered by J. S. Bach, but common to music
written for violin and viola da gamba generally and used
effectively by others as well. I am speaking of the unilinear
polyphony of Bach's unaccompanied suites for violincello,
his unaccompanied sonatas and partitas for violin, and a
number of lesser seventeenth- and eighteenth-century pieces
for the same instruments. The illusion of simultaneity is a
musical procedure as well. The creation of a "semblance of
polyphony," the generation of polyphony out of the instrument's own resources, was a common task of the gambist
in Sterne's time, so that Sterne's achievement in *Tristram
Shandy* (and the achievement of counterpoint in literature
generally) may be regarded as a literary counterpart of
Bach's determination to force polyphony out of a solo instrument. The novel, indeed any literary genre, is in effect
a solo instrument, counterpoint in fiction an effort to compel
that instrument to transcend its limitations and produce
polyphonic effects within a single line—the sense of simultaneity within linear succession. In contrapuntal sequences
like the "Fragment" on whiskers, as in Bach's suites for
cello, a bass note is periodically repeated or progressively
varied in rapid alternation with the melodic line that weaves
around or floats above it. The illusion of simultaneity arises
from the mind's encouraged tendency to trick itself into an
illusion that each line persists through the intervals during

which it has in fact been compelled to make way for the other. Sterne's technique, in other words, like that of others after him, need not be viewed as a grand but futile effort to imitate the inimitable musical capacity for simultaneity. It may also be taken—more modestly but not unrealistically —as a quite successful adaptation of an equally legitimate if less common procedure of baroque composition: unilinear counterpoint. The illusion of simultaneity imitates the illusion of simultaneity.

The "Fragment" and the sermon are unmistakably musical and polyphonic, but on occasion Tristram is even more explicit, naming his procedure as he goes. Perhaps the clearest example is the comic duet in which Dr. Slop damns Obadiah with the reading of Ernulphus's curse in one voice while uncle Toby whistles his "Lillabullero" in the other as contrapuntal "accompaniment" to and comment on the absurdity of the doctor's performance and the curse itself. "Dr. *Slop* wrapt his thumb up in the corner of his handkerchief, and with a wry face, though without any suspicion, read aloud, as follows,——my uncle *Toby* whistling *Lillabullero*, as loud as he could, all the time" (3:10.170). What follows, in facing pages of Latin and English, suggesting perhaps a further orchestration of the piece, is the reading of the highly repetitive incantation punctuated by uncle Toby's whistling—first "as loud as he could," then "not quite so loud as before," and climaxing with a "monstrous, long loud Whew——w——w——." Shortly before the end, "my uncle *Toby*, taking the advantage of a *minim* in the second barr of his tune, kept whistling one continual note to the end of the sentence——Dr. *Slop* with his division of curses moving under him, like a running bass all the way" (3: 11.171, 175, 177).

What we have is Sterne's literary version of the divisions he played on the bass viol. Divisions, or breaking the notes of the "ground" into more diminutive notes, was one of the most popular methods of accompanying on a figured bass, a commonplace sixteenth- and seventeenth-century composition and an essential component of Italian music through most of the eighteenth as well. It was also one of the brightest ornaments in the gambist's crowded bag and the subject of a number of technical treatises, Christopher Simpson's *The Division Viol* principal among them. Simpson lists five ways of breaking the ground, two of which are especially pertinent to Sterne's practice in *Tristram Shandy*. The third is "when the Minute Notes are employed in making a Transition to the next Note of the Ground . . . where Notes are broken to all the several distances both ascending and descending." In the fifth, "the said Minutes make a gradual Transition into some of the Concords, passing from thence, either to end in the sound of the holding Note, or else moving on to meet the next Note of the Ground." It is a matter, in other words, of transition, of process, not nearly so much what as how—how one gets from one place to another. Divisions permeate *Tristram Shandy*, offering one way, at least, to describe a fair measure of the novel's digressiveness—the practice of sustaining action in one of the novel's many time zones while breaking its subject into "more diminutive" parts that lead us first away and then back toward the underlying sequence, where we find the "divided" event either waiting impatiently in place or progressed to the next note of the ground.[5]

The voices in Sterne's composition are in contrapuntal relation to one another because human voices often are, but there is more to the achievement than the representation of simultaneity.[6] The "Fragment" on whiskers, the sermon on conscience, and the division on Ernulphus's curse share with the entire book a peculiar mixture of realism and formalism, verisimilitude and conscious artifice. I have spoken of simultaneity, and the achievement of simultaneity is perhaps the main source of sequences of this kind and of contrapuntalism in *Tristram Shandy*. Things go on together in the world and in the mind, people speak at once, and Tristram, dedicated to a representation of the way things are, works against the limitations of his medium toward the reproduction of reality. But that is only part of the explanation, for Tristram is no less dedicated to the moulding of life to art than to the creation of art as life. Human voices have been transformed into "voices" in a formal composition. The rapid alternation between voices, the juxtaposition of inner and outer world or of multiple inner and outer worlds, is a representation of simultaneous presence, but it is at the same time a complex artifice, a formal pattern of sound and visualized space whose shape, character, appeal, and effect cannot be accounted for—any more than in music—in exclusively representational terms.

This formalistic account is applicable not only to contrapuntalism in *Tristram Shandy*, but to its thematic structure as well: to the use of thematic fragmentation, combination, and variation; to transition, modulation, and repetition; and to the involuted concentricity of the novel's design. The forms experience takes—amorphousness is as creative a vision as any other—are patterned, heightened, and so illuminated. Formalism rises from, exceeds, and rejoins realism to create the curious world of *Tristram Shandy*.

The people in Tristram's world, then, are in contrapuntal relation to one another; but contrapuntalism is primarily a function of the complex relationship between past, present, and future, story, author, and reader. More specifically it is a product of the novel's digressiveness. It stems from the intrusions of Tristram-as-author into a tale ostensibly about his family and early years, and from the reciprocal intrusions of that history's own demands into the mind of the author. In an important sense the digressions are not intrusions at all since they are every bit as common and essential to the novel as the story he allegedly sets out to tell. Mendilow is right when he says that Tristram's comments should not be read as authorial intrusions since they are not extraneous to the book.[7] Tristram himself ostensibly regards them as intrusions since he treats them as interruptions, diagrams them as departures from the main road, and is as frustrated by their unavoidability as he is proud of their management. But that is only because Sterne is toying with a convention, the convention of linearity in fiction. Tristram's interruptions, in other words, are intrusions into the tale he allegedly wishes to tell, but utterly indispensable to the only tale he finally manages to communicate, the story of the mind. As in polyphonic music, the melodic lines are not in a proprietor-thief relationship, but in therapeutic partnership. The apparent abrasions, interferences, and conflicts may be personally frustrating, but they are essential to the growth of the business.

Actually, Tristram need not intrude at all to make his presence felt. In an important sense the adult Tristram, narrator of this wandering tale, is always present: the overall shape—or seeming shapelessness—of the narrative is a reflection of its unpredictable author and a consequence of the errant conditions of heredity, chance, and environment described in the narrative. These conditions insured that poor

Tristram would "neither think nor act like any other man's child."[8] The adult Tristram, then, is always implicitly there. Once he identifies and establishes himself as an authorial presence with his own separate character and quirks, his own problems and a second, more immediate tale to tell— the story of the writing of his book—Tristram assures his implicit but persistent presence in virtually every line he writes. We see every incident, transition, digression, and interpolation not only for what it intrinsically is, but at the same time as a sign of the author's character and temperament and as a manifestation, complication, or alleviation of his problem of authorship. In this sense his book may be said to be always implicitly contrapuntal: two distinct but related voices coexist on a single line.

In the absence of specific indicators, this is perhaps more theoretical than empirical, too subtle to be felt. But there is an abundance of more perceptible contrapuntalism in *Tristram Shandy*. We can begin with the concurrence of events within the "historical" world of the narration, a kind of magnified situational equivalent of the duet between whistle and curse.

As for my uncle *Toby*, his smoak-jack had not made a dozen revolutions, before he fell asleep also.——Peace be with them both. ——Dr. *Slop* is engaged with the midwife, and my mother above stairs.——*Trim* is busy in turning an old pair of jack-boots into a couple of mortars to be employed in the siege of *Messina* next summer,——and is this instant boring the touch holes with the point of a hot poker.——All of my heroes are off my hands;—— 'tis the first time I have had a moment to spare,——and I'll make use of it, and write my preface. (3:20.192)

Toby, Slop, and Trim are all simultaneously preoccupied. All coexist in the world of Tristram's past. Their activities are temporally concurrent though spatially separate, and while the novel, limited by printing conventions and reading habits, can only deal with them sequentially, Tristram does not allow us to forget the equally important temporal reality. They are all doing something quite different and in quite different places, but all at "this instant." This is simultaneity and simple enough. The complicating and contrapuntal element is introduced in the last sentence of the passage. With the intrusion of the narrator, enter the author side by side with his narration, the present side by side with the past, and the aesthetic world of the novel alongside the "historical" world of the Shandy family. They will all proceed together through the preface.

Here, in the relationship between narrator and narration, in the constant battle between plot and digression for space and attention, is the source of most of the novel's counterpoint. Tristram rarely achieves the kind of peaceful cooperation between story and digression he finds here, but he does maintain a kind of order within the chaos; even warfare has its rules. Beneath the seemingly amorphous flow run two persistent narrative strands which intertwine and, despite the temporal leaps, maintain an obscured but discernible chronology. The first deals primarily with Walter Shandy's household and with young Tristram—his conception, birth, and nose-smashing, his naming, window-sash circumcision, and consequent breeching. The second is concerned mainly with the campaigns of uncle Toby and his amours with Widow Wadman. These are the veins from which Tristram mines his digressions. Of course he cannot literally keep both his main plot and his digressions moving simultaneously before his reader's eyes. But Tristram, very much aware of the problem, constantly juggles the two lines of movement, bringing first one, then the other into view, and repeatedly reminds us that the events he has digressed from have not squealed to a halt simply because he has temporarily turned his attention elsewhere. Characters, once created or recreated, take on lives of their own and insist on living them whatever else an author may have in mind. Occasionally they are at rest, as when Tristram prepares to write his preface; but the preface is so long overdue (he is already half-way through the third volume) precisely because things do not often stand still for him. His heroes are rarely off his hands; rather they insistently crowd in on him, demanding their place in the narrative and impatiently elbowing their way back into line.

Take, for example, this account of uncle Toby's and Trim's approach to Widow Wadman's house that begins their amorous "siege" of the widow and her maid: "As Mrs. *Bridget*'s finger and thumb were upon the latch, the Corporal did not knock as oft as perchance your honour's taylor." This is as far as Tristram gets with his characters in this chapter, for at this point he jumps, by association, to himself: "I might have taken my example something nearer home; for I owe mine, some five and twenty pounds at least, and wonder at the man's patience." He then embarks on an explanation of his philosophy of "keeping straight with the world," his Rousseauian natural simplicity and economy. "True philosophy," he congratulates himself; but having done so he leaves off, responding to the persistent tug of his narrative: "but there is no treating the subject whilst my uncle is whistling *Lillabullero*.——Let us go into the house" (9:17.619–20).

Here as elsewhere, Tristram rapidly vacillates between the story he has ostensibly set out to tell and the only one he ever really tells at all, the story of his own mind and opinions. Rapid alternation has evolved into the standard device for suggesting simultaneous action, used effectively by Aiken, Huxley, Joyce, Flaubert in the famous auction scene of *Madame Bovary*, and a long list of others. But Sterne goes a bit beyond it. He cannot present simultaneity directly, but he can at least verbally suggest it. He can indicate to the reader what he cannot quite show him (love to though he would): that the story he is supposed to be telling and the story of the teller are going on together. The last lines of the passage above illustrate the technique, for they bring in a new event, one which is taking place on the narrative line, and present it as if it had been going on throughout the personal digression. "There is no treating the subject whilst my uncle is whistling *Lillabullero*," he sighs, and the obvious implication is that the two events were occurring together.

The special cause and quality of uncle Toby's whistling enriches the counterpoint. Toby only whistles his "Lillabullero" in response to the ineffably absurd, and in Tristram's typically punning fashion the whistling has two simultaneous applications. Toby himself is responding to the absurdity of his amorous "attack" on Mrs. Wadman, but as Tristram's reaction testifies, the whistling is equally applicable to his own philosophical pretensions. Hence, like counterpointed melodies, plot and digression are independent and contrasted on the one hand, complementary and related on the other. They are contrasted in their respective reference to different times (past and present), places (the physical world and the narrator's memory), characters (uncle Toby and Tristram), subject matters (love and "philosophy"), and modes of presentation (dramatic and expository). And they are related, not only by the initial association that bridged the contrasts and opened the sequence, but by their shared absurdity and by the presence of a common element or motive, the whistling of "Lillabullero" that affirms that key and rounds it off.

Author and tale, opinion and narration, digression and plot wind their way separately yet together. There is no presenting them in the full force of their simultaneous presence, but there is really no disentangling them either. The result is a complex contrapuntal texture that puts special burdens on reader and narrator alike, but offers at least the latter a very special satisfaction. Because of his book's insistent digressiveness,

the more your worships read, the more your worships will have to read.
 Will this be good for your worships eyes?
 It will do well for mine; and, was it not that my OPINIONS will be the death of me, I perceive I shall lead a fine life of it out of this self-same life of mine; or, in other words, shall lead a couple of fine lives together. (4:13.286)

Tristram is indeed leading a couple of fine lives together, but the satisfactions of complication are matched by its frustrations. Occasionally the contrapuntal texture of one or both lines of the narrative thickens to an almost unmanageable density. His mind floods with the images of its obligations clamoring for recognition and vying with the continuing demands of those already given life:

My mother, you must know,——but I have fifty things more necessary to let you know first,——I have a hundred difficulties which I have promised to clear up, and a thousand distresses and domestic misadventures crouding in upon me thick and three-fold, one upon the neck of another,——a cow broke in (to-morrow morning) to my uncle *Toby's* fortifications, and eat up two ratios and half of dried grass, tearing up the sods with it, which faced his horn-work and covered way.——*Trim* insists upon being tried by a court-

martial,——the cow to be shot,——*Slop* to be *crucifix'd,*——
myself to be *tristram'd,* and at my very baptism made a martyr of;
——poor unhappy devils that we all are!——I want swaddling,
——but there is no time to be lost in exclamations.——I have
left my father lying across the bed, and my uncle *Toby* in his old
fringed chair, sitting beside him, and promised I would go back
to them in half an hour, and five and thirty minutes are laps'd already.——Of all the perplexities a mortal author was ever seen
in,——this certainly is the greatest,——for I have *Hafen Slawkenbergius's* folio, Sir, to finish——a dialogue between my father
and my uncle *Toby,* upon the solution of *Prignitz, Scroderus, Am-
brose Paræus, Ponocrates,* and *Grangousier* to relate,——a tale out
of *Slawkenbergius* to translate, and all this in five minutes less, than
no time at all;——such a head!——would to heaven! my enemies
only saw the inside of it! (3:38.235)

The distresses, difficulties, and misadventures rise up out
of the memory, the Lockean warehouse of stored "ideas"
contesting with each other but cooperating in a joint assault
on the author's mind and story. They are all there together,
images out of the many-layered past, climbing over each
other's backs to get through the gates of the present, un-
willing to go single file up the narrow path traditional
fiction has cut for them. And to complicate matters further
still, there is Walter lying across his bed, very much a part
of the ongoing present and knocking from within. Like
the difficulties and distresses, Walter will have to wait—
this is fiction, not music, and we can read but one line at a
time—but Tristram insists on at least our awareness of the
density of his experience. If we saw the inside of his head
we would witness the multiple bombardment. Without a
cranial Momus glass, this will have to do.

We have come beyond the relative simplicity of the preparation for the preface and even of "Lillabullero" to a far
denser texture. But a couple of lives, however compressed,
are less than the full achievement. On at least one celebrated

occasion Tristram calls attention to the introduction of a third voice into his polyphonic scheme. In *The Young Joseph*, Mann tells us that Joseph's actual thoughts "were not with these mechanical and superficial prayers and lamentations but far below them, while lower down again were others yet more real, like their undertones and ground basses, so that the whole was like a moving music, perpendicularly composed, which his spirit was occupied in conducting on all three levels."[9] In volume 7, chapter 28, Sterne constructs a comparable three-tiered musical model of experience, though the depths of the strata are measured primarily in terms of time rather than profundity of feeling. Three layers of experience are compressed into a single complex moment. There is the adult Tristram journeying through France in flight from death; there is the younger Tristram on his grand tour, travelling much the same route some fifty years before (a recollection within a recollection); and there is Tristram Shandy, author, musing and writing about both, making plans for the future, and reflecting on his present state. Past, present, and future, multiple recollection, experience and anticipation, history, perception, and reflection all coexist and interact with one another in the narrator's hyperactive consciousness. Child, dying traveller, and rhapsodizing author exist together on the crowded page. With a mixture of wonder and forgivable pride, Tristram comments on the polyphonic texture of his piece:

——Now this is the most puzzled skein of all——for in this last chapter, as far at least as it has help'd me through *Auxerre*, I have been getting forwards in two different journies together, and with the same dash of the pen——for I have got entirely out of *Auxerre* in this journey which I am writing now, and I am got half way out of *Auxerre* in that which I shall write hereafter——There is but a certain degree of perfection in every thing; and by pushing at something beyond that, I have brought myself into such a situation, as no traveller ever stood before me; for I am this moment walking across the market-place of *Auxerre* with my father and my uncle *Toby*, in our way back to dinner——and I am this moment also entering *Lyons* with my post-chaise broke in a thousand pieces—— and I am moreover this moment in a handsome pavillion built by *Pringello*, upon the banks of the *Garonne*, which Mons. *Sligniac* has lent me, and where I now sit rhapsodizing all these affairs.

——Let me collect myself, and pursue my journey. (7:28. 515–16)[10]

The important point is that this remarkable passage is but the fullest realization and self-conscious recognition of a pattern implicit everywhere: the super-imposition of mind, man, and complex narration, the concurrent interaction of the author as man and storyteller with the many stories he has to tell.

There is counterpoint, then, between characters and in the intricate relationships between author and tale, but that is still not the whole of it. Polyphony may also arise out of the interaction between writer and reader, reader and story, or all three together: "What a tract of country have I run! ——how many degrees nearer to the warm sun am I advanced, and how many fair and goodly cities have I seen, during the time you have been reading, and reflecting, Madam, upon this story!" (7:26.510). Again we begin simply—and complicate. The relationship between the author and his reader seems relatively simple here, but only because a latent difficulty has been overlooked. Tristram's book is a living thing or perhaps rather a storehouse of sleeping lives, a kind of Spiritus Mundi that yields forth its souls whenever Sir, Madam, or any of the rest of us pick it up. In one sense, the only one that really interests Tristram, Madam is reading *while* he is writing, remembering, or living his life. Tristram's teeming life is counterpointed against our own more measured, relatively (but by no means totally) passive involvement. The two lines may seem to keep abreast of one another, but only if the narrator chooses to ignore the inherent inequity. Reading time and clock time in fact rarely correspond. If history is viewed panoramically the time required to read about it will be but a fraction of time accounted for; if meticulously set forth, either moment by moment or interrupted by time-consuming (our time) digressions, the other way round. If there is a principle at work here it is that of preestablished discord, and while Tristram, in a rare permissive mood, skips past the discrepancy this time through, he is usually, to his sorrow, more attentive. The absence of synchronization is inevitable but troublesome, and it leads him from ingenious evasion to glorious invention. Early in volume 2, Tristram is up against it. Only a little over two minutes of actual plot time have elapsed between the order to Obadiah to fetch Dr. Slop and his return with the man-midwife in tow; but the trip from Shandy Hall to Slop's house is some eight miles ride, and the horses of this world simply will not go that fast. Tristram's first answer to the discrepancy is a reconciliation through reading time. Obadiah may scarcely have had time to leave the house in terms of plot time, but measured against the reader's clock he has had time to spare: "It is about an hour and a half's tolerable good reading since my uncle Toby rung the bell, when *Obadiah* was order'd to saddle a horse, and go for Dr. *Slop*, the man-midwife;——— so that no one can say, with reason, that I have not allowed *Obadiah* time enough, poetically speaking, and considering the emergency too, both to go and come;———tho', morally and truly speaking, the man, perhaps, has scarce had time to get on his boots" (2:8.103). But the answer is strained, half-hearted, and only partly to the point, and it will not answer the pedantically scrupulous. Should the critic persist, however, Tristram is ready, and his defense leads him into the final complication: a three-part invention that engages reader, author, and characters in complex interplay and affirms his belief in the ultimate primacy of psychological time and aesthetic integrity:

> If the hypercritic will go upon this; and is resolved after all to take a pendulum, and measure the true distance betwixt the ringing of the bell, and the rap at the door;——and, after finding it to be no more than two minutes, thirteen seconds, and three fifths,—— should take upon him to insult over me for such a breach in the unity, or rather probability, of time;——I would remind him, that the idea of duration, and of its simple modes, is got merely from the train and succession of our ideas,——and is the true scholastic pendulum,—— and by which, as a scholar, I will be tried in this matter,——abjuring and detesting the jurisdiction of all other pendulums whatever.
>
> I would, therefore, desire him to consider that it is but poor eight miles from *Shandy-Hall* to Dr. *Slop*, the man-midwife's house;——and that whilst *Obadiah* has been going those said miles and back, [actually he "had not got above threescore yards from the stableyard"], I have brought my uncle *Toby* from *Namur*, quite across all *Flanders*, into *England*:——That I have had him ill upon my hands near four years;——and have since travelled him and Corporal *Trim*, in a chariot and four, a journey of near two hundred miles down into *Yorkshire*;——all which put together, must have prepared the reader's imagination for the entrance of Dr. *Slop* upon the stage,——as much, at least (I hope) as a dance, a song, or a concerto between the acts. (2:8.103–4; brackets mine)

The problem is physically insuperable. The reader has been reading some ninety minutes. Obadiah has in fact been gone hardly more than two. And in the remaining eighty-seven minutes plus, Tristram has taken us through more than four years in the life of uncle Toby, sick and well. The ordinary pendulum tells the ruin of the contrapuntal edifice

Tristram builds against all odds; every swing threatens to send more of it crumbling. But psychological time can manage, can account for, what clock time cannot. Such wonders of simultaneity are possible only in the mind. The structure of the novel, like its materials and subject, is the structure of mind. It is built and possible only there.

*Tristram Shandy* is a four-tiered model, a mainly polyphonic composition in four voices. In the bass, functioning as a kind of *cantus firmus* (fixed song) or ground bass, is the narrative plot, made up of a few basic motives or themes —Tristram's conception, his birth and nose-smashing, his naming and window-sash catastrophe—punctuated and ultimately succeeded by uncle Toby's adventures on the bowling green and his amours with the Widow Wadman. The principal function of this melody or melodic chord progression (more nearly the latter since the plot alone is more a matter of intermittently spaced blocks than continuous flow) is basically the function of the *cantus firmus* in medieval music and of its seventeenth- and eighteenth-century ancestor, the ground bass: to supply motivic materials for melodic expansion[11] and to provide a binding element of rational structure that would release the invented melodies accompanying it to expand in a free and improvisatory way.[12]

The second voice and principal accompanying melody, first forcing itself on our attention in volume 1, chapter 4, but present from the opening words and everywhere, belongs to the narrator himself. It is the melody of Tristram as adult, the man who, among a variety of other activities, is writing a book.

Good polyphonic music is vertical as well as horizontal, just as well-written harmony exhibits a strong sense of linearity along with its more important harmonic structure. "In the balance of lines, at once independent and dependent, forming a larger whole, yet each contributing its perfect wholeness, is the essence of counterpoint."[13] What this means is that while the basic structure of contrapuntal music is not dependent on the chords produced by the meetings of the separate melodies, the two voices must complement and relate meaningfully to one another. The chords are arrived at horizontally, melodically, but they are of vital importance to the music. Sitting at his desk, writing his book, Tristram is leading a life independent of the one he describes, or almost. He is an adult, his subject a child (when he is finally born), and there are years and miles and masses of experience between them. One has barely come into the world; the other knows he is on his way out. At the same time, though, and for both glaring and subtle reasons, he is leading, as he says, his two lives "together," and the inevitable meetings are crucial. The story of the author and of the writing of his book, is both independent and dependent, horizontal and vertical. It has its own separate chronology and its own peculiar problems, events, and resolutions, but it is intimately connected with, even in a sense derived from, the narrative in two ways. First, since the nature of the narrator and consequently his narrative style is the consequence of many of the events that comprise the plot (mainly but not exclusively his conception), the narrative provides the explanation for both. And second, while Tristram does have his own private adult life to lead—as we see mainly in the seventh volume—most of the life he leads before our eyes is an authorial life and as such is inseparable from its subject. The thematic materials of the plot provide both resource and impetus for many of the author's philosophical digressions, while the problems of its telling bear a comparable relation to his self-conscious reflections on authorship. The "life" of Tristram Shandy is the cause of his difficulties and the spur to his opinions.

The relationship is reciprocal, the intimacy, of course, mutual. The narrative too, while a separable story in its own right, is more separable than separate and finally less separable than one might imagine. It too develops partly in response to associations begun by the narrator, but more important its very shape and special character, its strange and erratic structure, is a product of the personality of the author (the creation of its own creation), and the events that make up the biographical plot—conception, nose-smashing, naming, and so on—are presented in an attempt to explain that personality. They tell us why he thinks, acts, and above all writes like no other man's child. The two lives, then, go their private ways. Each comes from somewhere and is going somewhere else when the meeting ends, but they are coming in a very important sense from each other, and that is where they are going back to as well.

Each voice, then, despite its essential independence, complements and in some sense springs from, even depends upon, the other. But while Tristram-as-author is inevitably more persistently "there," must, as he says, accompany us to the end of the work, it is the story of young Tristram more than that of the man writing at his desk that provides the structural frame, the element of "rational structure" in the novel. Ultimately, of course, it is the mind of the author that holds it all together, if anything does. But that mind is all-inclusive, includes both memory and present experience, and of the two it is the recollected tale that provides the base of operations and whatever sense of "home" the digressive structure permits. It is from one or another of the five or six principal events that make up the plot that most of the digressions—including some of the self-conscious reflections of Tristram-as-writer—begin their journeys and take their equipment, and it is to these that they ultimately return. "Slawkenbergius's Tale" is typical. A tale one could hardly call integral to the story of young Tristram, it nonetheless does owe its telling to that story. Tristram tells it because his father, a kind of nasal-compulsive obsessed with noses, translated it. His interest, in turn, is a result of an unfortunate tradition of short noses in the Shandy family which, in its turn, we learn of because Tristram's nose was smashed on delivery—and with that we are back to the ground bass of the book. Pick up the thread almost anywhere you like. Follow it back long and diligently enough and you will most often find its source in one of the germinal incidents in the narrator's biography.

The second independent and accompanying melody, the third voice, belongs to the reader. The reading of the book is a coherent, self-contained experience in itself, with its own beginning, middle, and end, and its own spatiotemporal locus, its own rhythms, problems, tensions and resolutions. But just as Tristram is leading his two lives together, the reader is leading his together with both, and the accompaniment is both parallel and interactive. Whatever may happen in eternity, parallel lines do meet in music. The reader, after all, is reading this book, and to read a book by Tristram Shandy is to accompany it almost literally through space and time. Tristram identifies and addresses us, invites us to know him and watch him work, and demands that we pay careful attention to the story he tells. He tries to synchronize the reader's time with that of his tale and to adapt our rhythms perfectly to his. When the attempt breaks down he makes the necessary apologies and compensations. When the failure is on our side, when Madam's attention slips, he sends her back to read the whole chapter again (as though there were two dots before the double bar), explains himself to the rest of us while she does, and welcomes her back when she returns. The reader inevitably goes his way, but he is basically an accompanist and makes, as he goes, his harmonic and rhythmic adjustments to the principal melodies.

The fourth voice is that of the rounded, self-contained digressions and interpolations; they exist in a time zone of their own, usually the more distant past. The stories of uncle Toby's wound and of his generosity to the fly, of aunt Dinah and the coachman, and of Yorick and his horse; set pieces like "Slawkenbergius's Tale," the preface, and the dedication; virtuoso display pieces like the "Fragment" on whiskers, the reading of the curse, Toby's panegyric on soldiery, Walter's and Trim's "harangues" upon death, Yorick's troped sermon on conscience—these and scores of others like them are the "decorations" of the piece, the shorter melodies, themes, variations, divisions, and transitions seventeenth- and eighteenth-century performers and composers used to decorate the ground bass, *cantus firmus*, or other melodies. These are the principal embellishments —sometimes running simultaneously with other melodies (polyphonic), sometimes merely taking off from a single, unreturning element, ornamenting and alternating with it (homophonic), and they are, as Tristram insists, "the sunshine . . . the life, the soul of reading."

If we are looking for a strict formal analogue for Sterne's book we will be disappointed, though we will deserve our disappointment. *Tristram Shandy* is not a ritornello or early contrapuntalized sonata, though, as we shall see, it does exhibit a kind of rudimentary ABA form. Nor is it a fugue, though it has many fugal elements. It has four voices; it evolves through a process of continuous expansion; it has a subject announced on the opening pages (the conception and victimization of the hero), a countersubject introduced contrapuntally in chapter 4 (the writing of the book), and a number of what may without strain be called "episodes." In the fugue, the function of an episode is to connect the recurring entrances of the subject, to divert attention from the theme, providing both variety and relief from it and thereby preparing us for its reentry. Most often the fugal episode is an expansion of one or more of the motives that make up the subject or countersubject, and it is characterized by sequential repetition and dialogue between voices. In almost every respect, this is a surprisingly faithful description of a number of the digressive episodes of *Tristram Shandy*, principally the "Fragment" on whiskers, the reading of Ernulphus's Curse, and Trim's systematically punctuated set orations: "The story of the king of Bohemia and his seven castles," the "harangue" on death, and his reading of Yorick's sermon on conscience.

   *Tristram Shandy* is in many respects fugal, but it is by no means a fugue; it is much too wild and loose to be. Not surprisingly, if a musical analogue is to be found at all, it will be found in one of the "free forms," loosely structured, often improvisatory pieces like the capriccio or any of the various types of preludes or fantasies popular in Sterne's time. Free forms are often used in music written to accompany or embellish an extramusical text—chorales, arias, and cantatas, for example—the demands of the text straining irresistibly against the constrictions of predetermined form. And what is true of music itself is more than a little likely to be true of its adaptation to fiction. More recent writers have used some of the so-called "fixed" musical forms as writing models—generally fugue or sonata—but most often either in relatively short works or in parts of longer ones. Critical efforts to demonstrate that works like *Ulysses* or *Remembrance of Things Past* are in their entirety covert sonatas are unpersuasive.

*Tristram Shandy* may be described, fairly I think, as a loosely-structured, strongly contrapuntal composition, marked by the free, expansive, and often dazzling improvisation of variations and embellishments over, under, and around a fixed sequence which it often obscures. So may a good deal of early eighteenth-century music—most evidently, perhaps, the fantasy. In the fantasy, as Felix Salzer points out, improvisation "implies the use of complex and large-scale prolongations which are organized so as to give the impression that the expected is to be avoided and that any effect of oneness or of one long sentence shall be eliminated. . . . [T]he Fantasy employs all creative means to stress change and variety in spite of an underlying structural framework. The Fantasy is organized improvisation."[14] Another analogous form, though usually in a more sedate tempo, is the chorale prelude, which often used the chorale melody as a *cantus firmus* and embroidered the theme, complicated the accompanying harmonies and polyphonic melodies, or even spun a kind of fugal structure around the basic tune of the chorale.[15] Any number of organ and clavier preludes and fantasies such as Bach's B-flat Major Prelude from *The Well-Tempered Clavier*, his Chromatic Fantasy and Fugue, or the G minor organ Fantasy and Fugue also fit the pattern, but perhaps the least strained analogue is the chorale concertato, where the *cantus firmus*, theoretically the unifying element of the piece, was barely perceivable as such; it was usually cut up into phrases (the five or six major events of the plot), each of which was given its own separate contrapuntal elaboration.

Whatever its validity, any analogy drawing formal lines across the arts will inevitably show signs of stress if pulled too tight. We are talking of procedures, not strict forms; of parallels and influences, not plaster casting; and the important point is this: the stories Tristram wants to tell are often simultaneous in his mind, and while he cannot present them synchronically, he can do his best to suggest their concurrence. The mind, like the world, works this way. It is not a unilinear stream of neatly outlined sequences but a sea of waves tumbling over and becoming one another. If Tristram is to present an accurate account of mind (at least his own) and world he must come to grips with the intractable fact of simultaneity. By doing so musically, by writing in effect a free form of polyphonic fiction, he achieves a number of compatible results: first, of course, the desired sense of mental and physical simultaneity, the richly woven texture of human experience; second, the pervasive sense of fluidity and constant motion; third, elements of rational structure and procedural familiarity and order to bank the flooding stream of consciousness; and finally, an indefinable, reverberative complex of feelings and responses that come, almost unavoidably, with the suggestion of a musical presence.

# 4

## The Treatment of Themes: Exposition, Development, and Recapitulation

The musical treatment of themes is if anything a more common literary phenomenon than counterpoint. In its simplest form, straight variation, as in Shakespeare's "That Time of Year," it is as indigenous to poetry as to music, and it carries no identifiably musical weight. In its more complicated forms and more recent adaptations, however, it is often quite distinctly musical. A poem, claimed Mallarmé, is a "geometry of phrases" arranged not logically but "symphonically" for the gradual evocation of a state of mind. Thomas Mann, musicalizing Fielding, spoke of the "epic prose-composition" as "a weaving of themes, . . . a musical complex of associations." In *Point Counter Point* and *The Counterfeiters* the traditional plot is replaced in large part by the pervasive modulation and variation of central themes, in Joyce's *Ulysses* and Woolf's *Mrs. Dalloway* by their symphonic elaboration and interaction. And Proust's *Remembrance of Things Past*, as one writer observed, is "a Symphony of Time, with themes stated, developed, and resolved in the manner of a composer rather than a narrator."[1]

Reasons for adopting a musical patterning of themes vary with author and time. The musical treatment may be simply a ready source of rational structure or a source of analogic support for an already existing structure: "The

novel as Mr. Wells long ago told me," wrote Ford Madox
Ford, "can very well be based on the structure of the Sonata!
*First Subject* Hero; *Second Subject* Heroine; *Re-statement*
of Case of Hero; ditto of Heroine; the *Free Fantasia* or mix-
up of the affairs of Hero and Heroine; the *Recapitulation* or
Marriage in which the themes of Hero and Heroine are re-
stated in one and the same key."[2] Frequently it is a means,
as for Mallarmé, of evoking vague musical associations,
achieving poetic "inclosure," or evoking states of mind.
Most commonly, as for Joyce and Proust, it is an image not
of *states* of mind, but of the mind's patterns and fluid
processes: the association, alternation, overlapping, integration, and repetition of ideas in the mind. For Marcel and
for Leopold Bloom, reality often assumes the form of a
complex of interrelated themes symphonically rather than
logically arranged; Tristram's mind makes a similar composition of the world.

Thematic development is in a sense as natural and indispensable to the novel as language, character, and action. But
Tristram has vowed to "follow no man's rules who ever
lived," and one of the most puzzling and disturbing consequences of his perverseness is his frustrating refusal to follow the traditional literary "rules" of thematic development.
Sterne shared with Proust the belief "that the subject is a
matter of indifference and that the mind can put anything
into it." Because they embody the fluid shapes of consciousness which his book is finally about, patterns of internal
relation, interaction, and organization are Tristram's first
concern. The independent significance and implications of
his themes—their "meanings" as correspondences to another reality—are less important than their potential for

development. Theme in *Tristram Shandy* is a matter not primarily of meaning but of use, not a question of secretion and accrual toward an organic unity of thought and perception, but of relationship, variation, and expansion. As in music, themes, subjects, or ideas are raised, turned over in the hand, held up to the light of Tristram's kaleidoscopic mind, explored, weighed with other related or contrasted themes, rubbed and played against them, and set down for a while only to be raised again in the same or altered form further on, held up to different lights, joined with new ideas, turned in new directions, set down again, and returned for a final showing at the end. Theme in *Tristram Shandy* is less what than how, less designation than passage, direction, and procedure; and the procedure in this case is an enveloping pattern of exposition, development, and return. Sterne's claim to impetuous originality needs qualification. He is following the rules of no novelist who had ever lived before him, but of virtually every composer of his time.[3]

---

## *Exposition*

The opening chapter of the novel is a miniature *Swann's Way*, Proust's "overture" to *Remembrance of Things Past*. It functions as introduction to some of the principal inhabitants of Tristram's world—Tristram himself as both seed and developed product, his mother and father, and the reader (uncle Toby appears first in chapter 3)—but far more important, it introduces most of the novel's principal themes. It is brief enough to reproduce in full:

I wish either my father or my mother, or indeed both of them, as they were in duty both equally bound to it, had minded what they were about when they begot me; had they duly consider'd how much depended on what they were then doing;—that not only the production of a rational Being was concern'd in it, but that possibly the happy formation and temperature of his body, perhaps his genius and the very cast of his mind;—and, for aught they knew to the contrary, even the fortunes of his whole house might take their turn from the humours and dispositions which were then uppermost:——Had they duly weighed and considered all this, and proceeded accordingly,——I am verily persuaded I should have made a quite different figure in the world, from that, in which the reader is likely to see me.——Believe me, good folks, this is not so inconsiderable a thing as many of you may think it;——you have all, I dare say, heard of the animal spirits, as how they are transfused from father to son, &c. &c.——and a great deal to that purpose:——Well, you may take my word, that nine parts in ten of a man's sense or his nonsense, his successes and miscarriages in this world depend upon their motions and activity, and the different tracks and trains you put them into, so that when they are once set a-going, whether right or wrong, 'tis not a halfpenny matter,——away they go cluttering like hey-go-mad; and by treading the same steps over and over again, they presently make a road of it, as plain and as smooth as a garden-walk, which, when they are once used to, the Devil himself sometimes shall not be able to drive them off it.

*Pray, my dear,* quoth my mother, *have you not forgot to wind the clock?*——*Good G—!* cried my father, making an exclamation, but taking care to moderate his voice at the same time,——*Did ever woman, since the creation of the world, interrupt a man with such a silly question?* Pray, what was your father saying?——Nothing. (1:1.4–5)

The chapter is quite literally seminal in a number of ways. It is about the conception of the hero, to be sure, but more than Tristram is begotten here. The important point is the unfortunate circumstances of the begetting and the darkened consequences such causes inevitably generate. His mother's poorly timed question about the clock, a symptom of her own associational enclosure, upset the delicate mechanism of conception and set the wheel of Tristram's fortune rolling inexorably in the wrong direction: uphill. Everything in the book is ultimately attributable to this misconceived conception—not simply because it began his journey through the world but because it dictated the nature of that journey. By guaranteeing that Tristram would "neither think nor act like any other man's child," it bears the responsibility for the erratic workings of both Tristram Shandy and *Tristram Shandy*.

But Tristram's conception is more than biologically, dramatically, and structurally generative. It is also the source—the "first spring" in the narrator's terminology—of most of the novel's major themes. Conception, sex, and birth are obvious and central, and we shall return to these. But there is also the theme of carelessness, misfortune, and victimization, introduced in his parents' failure to "mind what they were about when they begot me," and subsequently repeated in each of the major events of the autobiographical action: the smashing of his nose upon delivery, his damagingly misgiven name, and his near castration at the window. "But I was begot and born to misfortunes . . . ," Tristram sighs. "I was doom'd, by marriage articles, to have my nose squeez'd as flat to my face, as if the destinies had actually spun me without one" (1:15.41).[4]

The specific cause of the initial mishap during conception suggests other themes for future repetition, variation, and combination. The villain is Mrs. Shandy's interruptive question about the winding of the clock, and it is more fertile thematically than biologically. The clock suggests time,

another of Tristram's demons, the hastener of his death and
the nemesis of his autobiographical effort. Transience, simultaneity, mortality: these are the masks of time in the
novel, and each is fearsome subject of Tristram's reflections
about life and death, the plagues of authorship, and the
connection between them.[5]

Time is only one of the themes implicit in Mrs. Shandy's
question. Its asking, we learn in chapter 4, was the unfortunate end product of an associational coupling in Mrs.
Shandy's narrowly compassed mind. On the first Sunday of
every month, in order to get all the "little family concern-
ments" out of the way at one time, the aging Mr. Shandy
both wound the clock and bedded his wife. So naturally,
while he was engaged in the latter, his wife was reminded
of the former. That she was reminded is the result of the
association of ideas in the mind. That she raised the question
at such a moment is a mark of failed communication and
rapport owed to this habit of association and to the ultimate
entrapment of the mind in its private sphere. Between them,
the two occurrences introduce three more major and clearly
interrelated themes for future elaboration: the association
of ideas, the failure or absence of communication, and solipsism—all three essential to both the subject and the method
of the novel. This triangle points toward yet another theme
presented by implication in this case, in chapter 1: the
hobbyhorse. The hobbyhorse is Sterne's revised version of
the eighteenth-century master passion, the magnetic force
that draws all to it and the limit of whose reach defines the
limits of the perceptual and associational field of its rider,
locking him in the bounded world of the fixated imagination. Walter's hobbyhorse is obscure learning and odd hypotheses; Toby's and Trim's are soldiery and the bowling

green; Dr. Slop's is midwifery and Roman Catholicism; Mrs. Wadman's is marriage and sex. Tristram's is his book, and his own odd hypothesis about the effect of the animal spirits on character and destiny offered here in chapter 1 is later adapted to describe both his book and the hobby-horse in general: "when they are once set a-going . . . away they go cluttering like hey-go-mad; and by treading the same steps over and over again, they presently make a road of it." The parallel is no coincidence but the mark of con-sanguinity. The book is hobbyhorse; both are intimately related—one as product, one as part—to character in gen-eral; and all are determined by the dispensation of the animal spirits at the moment of conception. With this we are brought to the final theme, one of the most pervasive and important introduced in this remarkable exposition: the mechanistic relationship between mind and body.

Seven themes, then: (1) sex, conception, and birth; (2) carelessness and misfortune; (3) time; (4) the association of ideas; (5) failed or nonexistent communication; (6) solipsism and the hobbyhorse (warfare, odd learning, and authorship); (7) the relationship between mind and body. This matter set in Shandean motion is *Tristram Shandy:* the development of these themes via repetition, juxtaposition, variation, expansion, and interaction with each other and with other related or component themes and motives, gen-erates the novel. In a brief, seemingly quite simple, and bawdily comic opening chapter, Tristram has managed to tell us not only how he came to be, but how he came to be the strange sort of creature he has become, and how, by implication, he came to write the strange sort of novel we are about to read. And in the process, he makes that novel possible. In the act of describing the conception that gave him his life and special character, he plants the seeds whose cultivation gives life and special character to his book.

---

## *Development*

In the development section of a musical composition, the material may:

(a) be divided into smaller figures (this creates an effect of stretto, or compressed action, often leading to considerable extensions in structure, as in the beginning of the development section of the first movement of Mozart's Symphony no. 41); (b) have its motifs or figures regrouped into new phrases (this presents the original material in a new light, with a different rhetorical effect, as in the first movement of Beethoven's Symphony no. 8); (c) have the contour or character of its motifs altered (this often imparts a different expressive value to the original material, as in the fugato of the development of the first movement of Beethoven's Quartet in F major op. 18, no. 1); (d) be associated with harmonic explorations and digressions (this creates a sense of continuous and even unpredictable movement, and provides a basis for the use of a, b, and c.[6]

"Such harmonic activity can be found in virtually any development section of a classical or romantic sonata form,"[7] and the reader of *Tristram Shandy* will recognize them as the principal types of thematic activity in the novel as well. Themes are fragmented, regrouped with other themes or in new combinations, expressively altered or modulated, and sent off on digressive explorations of their rich and varied possibilities.

To describe the development and interaction of all the themes exposed in chapter 1 would be virtually to rewrite *Tristram Shandy* in infinitely less readable form. I shall content myself with some representative samplings of the major themes and developmental techniques Sterne employs, principally motivic fragmentation and regrouping, contrast, transition, modulation, and variation. It hardly matters where we begin, since everything will ultimately generate everything else, but the focal events of the autobiographical history should provide a fruitful starting point. These events—the delivery and nose-smashing, the naming, and the window-sash mishap—are, as I have said, the *cantus firmus* or basso ostinato of the piece, providing not only a framework for contrapuntal embellishment, but source material for the thematic development and elaboration that constitutes the novel.

## Fragmentation and regrouping

Each of these three germinal events is itself both consequence and further illustration of the opening theme of carelessness and misfortune, and each is both composed and productive of other themes announced in the exposition: Tristram's clumsy delivery—of birth, sex and impotence; his misnaming—of failed communication and the mind-body relationship; the window-sash accident—of sex, impotence, and war. All three also involve and develop out of the inherently related themes of hobbyhorses and the association of ideas. Potentially, at least, there is nothing distinctive here. Expansion and interrelationship of motives and themes is endemic to literature of any marked coherence and density. Certain images, subjects, and ideas will inevitably recur and, if the recurrence is sufficiently frequent and the work sufficiently coherent, they will begin to confront and interact with one another to form new and meaningful patterns. In conventional fiction, however, this sort of development is subordinate, supportive, often subliminal, occasionally incidental. In *Tristram Shandy* the developmental processes are, for one thing, distinctly musical; for another, they are very nearly all there is. They are the novel's substitute for plot and the conventional presentation of theme and idea; they are among the few materials of construction that in the absence of more traditional foundations hold the building together and allow it to grow; and, once the nature of the game comes clear, they begin to replace the more traditional elements of fiction as the principal object of the reader's attention.

For all the help Tristram offers us—much of it contradictory—we will never really know how *Tristram Shandy* was conceived or written. But a good guess, it seems to me, is that he worked along lines suggested by Mary Russell Mitford about a half-century later: "With regard to novels, I should like to see one undertaken without any plot at all . . . without any preconceived design further than one or two incidents and dialogues, which would naturally suggest fresh matter, and so proceed in this way, throwing in incident and characters profusely, but avoiding all stage tricks and strong situations."[8] My guess is that Sterne began with five major incidents in mind—Tristram's conception, birth, naming, and window accident, and the amours of uncle Toby and the widow Wadman—and, out of the themes and other incidents and characters these events suggested, improvised the rest in accordance with procedures of transition and expansion analogous to if not derived from musical composition. *Tristram Shandy* is matter in motion. The matter is characters, themes, and incidents chosen largely for their mobility and exploitability. The motion is musical.

One of the compulsions costliest to the success of Tris-

tram's enterprise is his insistence, as the opening chapter
testifies, on tracing things back to their radical beginnings.
It would be easy enough to begin with Tristram's birth and
nose-smashing and go on. But that is to overlook the endless
chain of causes that generate, mechanistically, the consequences that comprise his life, and it is not the Shandean
way. Even the conception is not quite the beginning. The
question that marred it must itself be accounted for, and it
is owed, like so much else, to the association of ideas in the
mind.[9] The same method is applied to his birth, though far
more elaborately, and what emerges is a tale woven out of
a complex of related themes and thematic fragments. In
order to account for the birth, Tristram must tell us the
story of the local midwife who will attend Mrs. Shandy—or
so we think at this point—and this leads him into the
linked history (a digression within a digression) of Parson
Yorick's own midwife practice. Here it merges with the related impotence theme—the practice left Yorick no time
to attend the impotent—a theme which likewise shows up
in a variety of other contexts, guises, and permutations (including the actual birth), and which achieves its climactic
expression at the end of the novel. When Tristram is finally
born, impotence, a hybrid offshoot of the sex and victimization themes announced in the exposition, links again with
birth through another subordinate and related theme, noses.
Poor Tristram's is smashed on delivery, and the sexual implication is clear. Tristram is at great pains to insure that by
noses he means precisely that—noses—and nothing else;
but he persists too much and quite deliberately presses for
the sexual innuendo in the act of disclaiming it. The crush-
ing of his nose is the unfortunate consequence of a chain of
events set going by the ominous circumstances of his con-

ception, a variant of the wound in uncle Toby's groin, and a presage of his own near castration at the window some years later.

But noses are more than mere sexual puns. They are a secondary theme in their own right, subject to development and elaboration, and almost as productive as birth. Tristram's damaged nose calls to his mind the quaint history of Shandean noses, which in turn had aroused Walter's special interest in this organ some years earlier and led him to translate Slawkenbergius's proboscular tales, one of which we are therefore treated to. All of these digressions, we should note, are elaborations of the nose theme first stated explicitly in the chronological tale of young Tristram but implicit in the sexual evasiveness and innuendo of chapter 1. Slawkenbergius's tales are themselves variations on the same theme. "In general," says Tristram, "they are to be looked upon by the learned as a detail of so many independent facts, all of them turning round somehow or other upon the main hinges of his subject, and collected by him with great fidelity, and added to his work as so many illustrations upon the doctrines of noses" (3:42.242). Five themes and subthemes, then, converge on Tristram's natal mishap: misfortune and carelessness, noses, odd learning (hobbyhorse), birth itself, and sex. And every one can be traced back, thematically as well as structurally, to the opening statement.

The naming of the hero, like virtually all else in *Tristram Shandy*, is there primarily for what can be done with it. Through the variations worked on it by Walter (1:19.55; 4:11.250), Tristram (4:21.299–300), and Trim and Toby (4:18.295), it develops into an important secondary theme. But names are suitable for more than variation. They are

also developed via association and integration with two of
the major themes of the novel: the mind-body relationship and the failure of communication. Walter's hypothesis
about the critical importance of names is counterpart to
Tristram's opening hypothesis about the comparable import
and influence of animal spirits. Both are affirmations of the
inseparability of body and soul, of the effect of the tangible
and physical on the mental and spiritual, evident everywhere in the novel. The "soul and body are joint-sharers
in every thing they get: A man cannot dress, but his ideas get
cloath'd at the same time" (9:13.616). And here is grist
for Tristram's endlessly grinding mill. Ideas are dressed,
opinions are apples, problems are knots, wit and judgment
are as two knobs on the back of a chair, a hinge is a connection, a mental set is a hobbyhorse, death is a man in pursuit,
a mood is a musical instrument or key, a marbled page is
"motley emblem of my work," and so it goes through a
hundred other hypostatizations. This is no mere frivolous
play, though Tristram has no argument with frivolity. "A
man's body and his mind, with the utmost reverence to both
I speak it, are exactly like a jerkin, and a jerkin's lining;
——rumple the one——you rumple the other" (3:4.
160). What happens on the outside, in other words, happens on the inside. Body is a key to mind, the physical to
the spiritual, and in the absence of Momus's glass, that direct
window on the soul, there is no shorter or straighter path
to the lining of character, spirit, thought, and fortune than
through the jerkin of the skin. And the relationship is reciprocal. The physical may be cause as well as sign and
consequence of the spiritual, and indeed most of the major
events in the novel can be traced to this theory of the inseparability of soul and body and the importance of the

body's fate to soul. Animal spirits transfused from father to son determine character and fortune, and each subsequent mishap is a major variation on the theme—at once consequence, sign, and further assurance that Tristram is doomed to remain the "Sport of small accidents."

Unhappy *Tristram*! child of wrath! child of decrepitude! interruption! mistake! and discontent! What one misfortune or disaster in the book of embryotic evils, that could unmechanize thy frame, or entangle thy filaments! which has not fallen upon thy head, or ever thou camest into the world——what evils in thy passage into it!——What evils since!——produced into being, in the decline of thy father's days——when the powers of his imagination and of his body were waxing feeble——when radical heat and radical moisture, the elements which should have temper'd thine, were drying up; and nothing left to found thy stamina in, but negations——'tis pitiful——brother *Toby*, at the best, and called out for all the little helps that care and attention on both sides could give it. But how were we defeated! You know the event, brother *Toby*,——'tis too melancholy a one to be repeated now, ——when the few animal spirits I was worth in the world, and with which memory, fancy, and quick parts should have been convey'd,——were all dispersed, confused, confounded, scattered, and sent to the devil. (4:19.296–97)

If there is one pervasive theme in this novel, one idea that can be said to provide anything even remotely reminiscent of thematic unity, it is this relationship between mind and body, one of the principal themes of the opening chapter and one of the prime movers of the fiction. It not only accounts for much of what takes place in *Tristram Shandy*, but can describe method and purpose as well. "True *Shandeism*," Tristram declares, "think what you will against it, opens the heart and lungs, and like all those affections which partake of its nature, it forces the blood and other vital fluids of the body to run freely thro' its channels, and makes the wheel of life run long and chearfully round" (4:32.337–38).

The object of Shandeism, and of the book, is to lighten and vitalize our tempers, and it is achieved mechanistically.

> If 'tis wrote against any thing,——'tis wrote, an' please your worships, against the spleen; in order, by a more frequent and a more convulsive elevation and depression of the diaphragm, and the succussations of the intercostal and abdominal muscles in laughter, to drive the *gall* and other *bitter juices* from the gall bladder, liver and sweet-bread of his majesty's subjects, with all the inimicitious passions which belong to them, down into their duodenums. (4:22.301–2)

The description is absurd, the purpose comic and satiric, but there is a crucial element of seriousness here, at least within the context of the fictive frame. The purpose of the book (says Tristram, if not Sterne) is to alter spirit by changing body, and in this most mechanistic of worlds where all is restless matter in continuous motion, physical effects are most directly achieved by markedly physical means. Ordinary descriptive language will not do, and Tristram has recourse to a variety of more tangible devices: physical gestures, changes of posture, illustrations and diagrams, marbled, blank, and blackened pages, hypostases, concrete analogies, hands, dashes, asterisks—and music. These are at once indices to the narrator's and his characters' minds and instruments for the manipulation of our own, and in one sense at least music—whether as metaphor, sound, or structural analogue—is best suited to his ends.

> For to say nothing of the havock, which by a certain consequence is unavoidably made by it all over the finer system of the nerves, which you know convey the animal spirits and more subtle juices from the heart to the head, and so on——It is not to be told in what a degree such a wayward kind of friction works upon the more gross and solid parts, wasting the fat and impairing the strength of a man every time as it goes backwards and forwards. (4:31.336)

What this passage (and a dozen others like it) makes clear is Sterne's at least ostensible adherence to the vibration theory of affect. It is the nerves, those indiscernible fibers of our being, that convey the animal spirits and subtle juices from heart to head and head to heart. And music, itself a system of harmonic vibrations, an aesthetic model of the harmonic condition of world and soul, and a symbolic form mirroring the motions of the inner life of man, plays—as eighteenth-century aestheticians repeatedly insisted—most directly and effectively on the central nervous system. As such it was the most affective of the arts, the aesthetic stimulus to which the nerves and therefore the passions and affections were most responsive.

We may round off our analysis of fragmentation and regrouping with a brief reference to the third catastrophe in the melodramatic life of the hero: the accident at the window. The incident is one of innumerable surfacings of the sex theme. Sex, a theme of major importance, occurs not only in connection with Tristram's conception, birth, and misfortune, but in the suggestiveness of whiskers, gashes, and fur caps as well as noses; it mingles with the omnipresent threat of impotence in the tale of Phutatorius and the boiling chestnut—where misunderstanding and failed communication is also at issue—in the wounds to Trim's knee and Toby's groin (wounds are an interesting minor theme), and in Obadiah's complaint about the impotent bull; and it becomes central in the account of Toby's amours with Mrs. Wadman on the bowling green. Sex likewise couples with the seemingly contrastive theme of war in a variety of ways: dramatically—Trim's eager search for material to help fortify the bowling green leads him to the window and results in the injury to Tristram's groin; punningly—the corporal's zeal is responsible for the fact that "nothing was well hung in our family"; and metaphorically—the Widow's seductive advances and uncle Toby's own more innocent responses are characterized as "attacks" and "sieges." Mrs. Wadman is possessed of "as venereal a pair of eyes" as Venus herself, and "An eye," as Tristram observes, "is for all the world exactly like a cannon"; it's the carriage that matters most. "These attacks of Mrs. *Wadman*" are, as Tristram says, "of different kinds; varying from each other, like the attacks which history is full of, and from the same reasons" (8:17.556). But attacks they are, and though Trim is convinced that love is a different thing from warfare, it proves less different than he or Toby might have hoped. Her question as to where Toby received the wound takes him back to the battle at the gate of St. Nicholas, but it takes the Widow directly to his groin; and when the disparity of interests is discovered the affair is at an end. Uncle Toby's amours, the much praised and repeatedly promised "tastiest morsel of the story," and the culmination of the theme of love, emerges as a new melodic line composed largely of the themes of sex, war, and failed communication.

The development of thematic material in *Tristram Shandy*—its repetition, fragmentation, and recombination is governed largely by the association of ideas in the mind. Noses suggest one thing to Tristram, another to Walter, still a third to uncle Toby; what they suggest suggests something else again to the galloping narrator, chronology yields to thematic expansion, and conventional autobiography is doomed. But to say that *Tristram Shandy* works by association is legitimate only if we expand that concept to include another major structural determinant in the book, the need to tell all—to explain incidents by going back to first causes or to extend meaning by broadening context, by connecting events and opinions to other events and opinions that light them up from every side. An incident is related, an attitude or opinion expressed, but this is only the beginning. The event is preposterous, the idea absurd, and as often as not both are intrinsically trivial. Meaning and value come from relation, context, and implication, from what went before and what comes after, from connections and trains of thought established in the narrator's mind and the complex pattern of their presentation. When Tristram begins to describe his birth and then realizes he must first tell about the midwife, Yorick, Dr. Slop, the lying-in contract, and so on, he is moved from point to point not by a verbal free association visualizable, perhaps, as a string of fuses and firecrackers, but by a train of thought more widely conceived to include an important element not of premeditation but of rational decision. He is not pulled inexorably by a chain of associations exploding in his mind, but driven by the desire to render the full complexity of both thought and world. The result is not "associationism" in its most restricted sense, but it is a pattern of mental connections and associations. And the result of that is an almost inevitable musicality of texture and form.

Whenever internal association replaces chronology and external reference as formal determinant, the novel begins its approach to the condition of music. This is one explanation for the pervasive musicality, deliberate or otherwise, of so much stream-of-consciousness fiction. "The musical idea," composer Roger Sessions writes, is "the element which gives the music its essential character, and . . . the starting point of a vital musical 'train of thought'" which "differs from any other train of thought only in the fact that its medium is tones, not words or images or symbols."[10] Actually, as Sessions himself remarks soon after, it differs in another sense as well. An important aspect of the associationism in *Tristram Shandy* is the emotive impulse behind a good deal of the associative movement of the novel. In this revolutionary approach to development and structure, Sterne is working in the rococo tradition of his contemporary C.P.E. Bach. Like Sterne, though a few years earlier, Bach introduced a strong personal and subjective element into composition and contributed to the advancement of an already growing tendency in instrumental music toward dependence on the composer's inner resources both for emotional intensity and the ordering of its emotions.[11] Association in *Tristram Shandy* is more than fortuitous psychological connection, more than the arousal in the mind of cause by effect or of one event or idea by another in some sense related to it. Indeed it is more than the association of abstract ideas. It may also be the association between feelings and emotions, whether by similarity, contrast, or some more mysterious relationship; and in this Sterne's technique is reminiscent not only of the music of C.P.E. Bach, but of musical motion in general.

A musical train of thought [writes Sessions] is in large measure actually a train of impulse or of feeling. This is also true of many nonmusical trains of thought; the ideas or images are highly charged with emotion, and emotion frequently motivates the sequence of ideas. But in music it is the logic of sensation and impulse that determines the ultimate validity of the train of thought and gives the musical work not only its expressive power but whatever really organic unity it may possess.[12]

Development by association, then, is inherently musical, development by impulse and feeling more distinctively so and particularly descriptive of the improvisational rococo style of composition contemporary with *Tristram Shandy* and similar to it in other ways as well. But the musicality of association in *Tristram Shandy* and in stream-of-consciousness fiction is not merely a matter of the presence of association or even of its characteristically emotive logic. To work by association, in anything but a perpetually and ultimately pointless linear way, is to work largely out of one's own internal and therefore relatively limited resources, and there are only so many things that can be done with the materials at hand. They can be repeated, expanded, combined, fragmented and recombined, repeated in a different tone or mood, spoken by or applied to different characters, set in different times, places, and contexts, and so on. And all have their counterparts in musical development. In other words, to work by association is to work by linkage, distortion, fragmentation, repetition, contrast, reformation, and combination; it is to work musically. Since music is fundamentally nonimitative, it is almost necessarily associational. It is the spider rather than the bee, spinning its home from within, and it has developed all the spider's devices. Whatever an author is likely to do along these lines, composers are likely to have done before.

## Modulation and variation

There is more to the musical treatment of themes in *Tristram Shandy* than their repetition, fragmentation and reformation, threading and weaving. There is also contrast, transition, variation, and modulation. Here is Aldous Huxley as Philip Quarles:

The musicalization of fiction. Not in the symbolist way, by subordinating sense to sound. (*Pleuvent les bleus baisers des astres taciturnes.* Mere glossolalia.) But on a large scale, in the construction. Meditate on Beethoven. The changes of moods, the abrupt transitions. (Majesty alternating with a joke, for example, in the first movement of the B flat major Quartet. Comedy suddenly hinting at prodigious and tragic solemnities in the scherzo of the C sharp minor Quartet.) More interesting still, the modulations, not merely from one key to another, but from mood to mood. A theme is stated, then developed, pushed out of shape, imperceptibly deformed, until, though still recognizably the same, it has become quite different. In sets of variations the process is carried a step further. Those incredible Diabelli variations, for example. The whole range of thought and feeling, yet all in organic relation to a ridiculous little waltz tune. Get this into a novel. How? The abrupt transitions are easy enough. All you need is a sufficiency of characters and parallel, contrapuntal plots. While Jones is murdering a wife, Smith is wheeling the perambulator in the park. You alternate the themes. More interesting, the modulations and variations are also more difficult. A novelist modulates by repudiating situations and characters. He shows several people falling in love, or dying, or praying in different ways—dissimilars solving the same problem. Or, *vice versa*, similar people confronted with dissimilar problems. In this way you can modulate through all the aspects of your theme, you can write variations in any number of different moods.[13]

If that was too long for you, Madam, and you skipped through or over it, go back and read it again, for it's all there. Quarles seems not to have known it, but there he sits in 1928, planning a musical novel his own creator managed only partially and imperfectly, but which had in fact been quite impressively achieved 150 years before. We can begin with the modulations, "not merely from one key to another, but from mood to mood."

One of the principal differences between the late baroque music contemporary with Sterne and the early baroque style is the fully realized tonality of the late baroque. The definitive realization of tonality in Italian music of the late seventeenth century marks the beginning of the gradual evolution from polyphonic music toward homophonic forms

that put far greater stress on a pervasive sense of key. Since
the new harmonic orientation was, in its early stages, bal-
anced by the melodic line provided by the continuo in the
bass, the result was a hybrid form of "luxuriant" counterpoint called "continuo-homophony" that began with Corelli
and culminated in the work of J. S. Bach.[14] Since *Tristram
Shandy* is both contrapuntal and homophonic and exhibits a
melodic bass line as well as a strong sense of tonality, one
might make a case for another analogue or historical source
in this prevalent new form, but my main concern is with
the broader point: the increased importance and awareness
of tonality in early eighteenth-century music and, consequently, of the modulations from key to key.

Key-change was not a mere structural or even an autono-
mously musical device. According to the doctrine of affections, certain keys were associated with certain affective
qualities identified with the ancient modes they were presumably derived from, and baroque treatises on music almost always contain lists explaining the affective qualities
of each mode or key.[15] That there is an affinity "between the
ancient modes and the modern keys," wrote Sir John Hawkins, "is beyond a doubt," and like the modes, "the several
effects of the modern keys are discoverable in the tendency
which each has to excite a peculiar temper or disposition of
mind."[16] Many eighteenth-century composers apparently
believed in these relationships between emotions and keys,
and especially in the composition of music to accompany
religious or other texts—the cantata, opera, and oratorio,
for example—at least ostensibly observed them.

So does Tristram. Modulation in *Tristram Shandy* takes
two principal shapes. The first lays stress on the actual
passage from one key to another rather than on achieved

modulation, derives unmistakably from the doctrine of affections, and is explicitly musical. It is Trim's way of telling a tale.

Since there is a discernible connection between key and mood, a story, if it is to have its proper emotive effect, must be told in the proper key, and Trim is the past master of tonality. Before beginning his never-to-be-finished story of the King of Bohemia and his seven castles, Trim must first hem twice "to find in what key his story would best go, and best suit his master's [uncle Toby's] humour" (8:19. 559). But Trim never gets beyond the first few lines of his narrative. Associations, whether his own or uncle Toby's, take him so far afield that the key is lost and the tale eventually abandoned. Trim has better luck with the story of his poor imprisoned brother Tom. As before, the constant interruptions drive Trim further away from the story's proper key. At one point, following a digressive discussion of the plight of the Negro, Trim tries to get back to his story. But alas, "by the many sudden transitions all along, from one kind and cordial passion to another, in getting thus far on his way, he had lost the sportable key of his voice which gave sense and spirit to his tale" (9:6.607). After two attempts to resume his story and two successive failures, Trim calls upon his mastery of the significant gesture, and a transition from one attitude to another succeeds where all else has failed. It resolves his discord into harmony, modulates him back to the proper key, and enables him to go on: "so giving a stout hem! to rally back the retreating spirits, and aiding Nature at the same time with his left arm a-kimbo on one side, and with his right a little extended, supporting her on the other—the Corporal got as near the note as he could; and in that attitude, continued his story"

(9:6.607).Trim's problem is microcosmic, his difficulties a patent corollary of Tristram's own narrative frustrations. Both are led astray by associations and the irresistible transitions from one passion to another; and Trim, no less than Tristram, knows the efficacy of modulatory transitions in resolving discord back into harmony and getting one's story told. If one kind of transition takes you off on a wild dance you never intended, another kind can dance you home, and somehow, between the two and with more than a little luck, the story will be told. Transitions, as the man said, are all in all.

The second modulatory technique is structural, more a matter of alternation and transposition than of gradual transition. It is also more pervasive, subtler, more complex, and the unmistakable ancestor of modulation in modern fiction. In the deft tailoring of his themes, as he tries them on contrasting sets of characters and views them from different angles and in different lights, Sterne introduces modulation to the novel, precisely in Huxley's terms. "A novelist," says Quarles, "modulates by repudiating situations and characters. He shows several people falling in love, or dying, or praying in different ways—dissimilars solving the same problem." Either this is an uncanny coincidence or Huxley has not given Sterne his due. "There is nothing," says Tristram, "shews the characters of my father and my uncle *Toby*, in a more entertaining light, than their different manner of deportment, under the same accident——" namely love. His father, though vulnerable to the passion before he married, would never submit to it. Instead, owing to a "subacid kind of drollish impatience in his nature . . . [he] would pish, and huff, and bounce, and kick, and play the Devil, and write the bitterest Philippicks against the eye that ever man wrote" (8:26.578–79).

My uncle *Toby*, on the contrary, took it like a lamb——sat still and let the poison work in his veins without resistance——in the sharpest exacerbations of his wound (like that on his groin) he never dropped one fretful or discontented word——he blamed neither heaven nor earth——or thought or spoke an injurious thing of any body, or any part of it; he sat solitary and pensive with his pipe——looking at his lame leg——then whiffing out a sentimental heigh ho! which mixing with the smoak, incommoded no one mortal.

He took it like a lamb——I say. (8:26.579)

In matters of love, Walter and Toby are not the only antithetical pair. The Widow's approach is quite different from either of their own. To her, love is neither philosophical rhetoric nor sentiment, but sensuality, possessiveness, and practicality, and it calls for neither irascible defensiveness nor passive acceptance, but for immediate, devious, and seductive action.

There is nothing in it out of doors and in broad daylight, where a woman has a power, physically speaking, of viewing a man in more lights than one——but here, for her soul, she can see him in no light without mixing something of her own goods and chattels along with him——till by reiterated acts of such combinations, he gets foisted into her inventory——

——And then good night. (8:8.546)

If Walter is all bluster and cynicism and Toby all innocence, the Widow is all calculation. Wheeling her venereal eyes about like cannons, she assaults Toby in his own sentry box. A deftly placed hand, a fortuitously stationed thigh, and the unsuspecting Toby is a smitten man.

Trim, the fourth major participant in the game, the fourth modulated variation on a theme, balances Toby's childish naiveté with somber sophistication. "I thought *love* had been a joyous thing, quoth my uncle *Toby*. 'Tis the most serious thing, an' please your honour (sometimes) that is in the world" (8:20.570). But Trim is more than a mere answer to Toby; he is something of a mixture of his master, the Widow, and Walter. His tale of his affair with the young Beguine mixes Walter's rhetorical genius with Toby's sentimentality and the Widow's salaciousness, and his coy confusion of love and sex is a comic illustration of Walter's unheeded warning to his brother.

She pass'd her hand across the flannel, to the part above my knee, which I had equally complained of, and rubb'd it also.
    I perceived, then, I was beginning to be in love——
    As she continued rub-rub-rubbing——I felt it spread from under her hand, an' please your honour, to every part of my frame——
    The more she rubb'd, and the longer strokes she took——the more the fire kindled in my veins——till at length, by two or three strokes longer than the rest—— my passion rose to the highest pitch——I seiz'd her hand——
    ——And then, thou clapped'st it to thy lips, *Trim*, said my uncle *Toby*——and madest a speech.
    Whether the corporal's amour terminated precisely in the way my uncle *Toby* described it, is not material; it is enough that it contain'd in it the essence of all the love-romances which ever have been wrote since the beginning of the world. (8:22.574–75)

As this interjected comment indicates, Tristram works his own modulations on the theme. At the end of the long passage from Quarles's notebook quoted above, Quarles suggests that the author can also modulate by assuming

the god-like creative privilege and simply elect[ing] to consider the events of the story in their various aspects—emotional, scientific, economic, religious, metaphysical, etc. He will modulate from one to the other—as, from the aesthetic to the physico-chemical aspect of things, from the religious to the physiological or financial. But perhaps this is a too tyrannical imposition of the author's will.

Some people would think so. But need the author be so retiring? I think we're a bit too squeamish about these personal appearances nowadays.[17]

Squeamishness was never one of Tristram's problems, and as any glance through his book will show, he assumes this god-like creative privilege everywhere and elects to consider the events of his story in almost every aspect Quarles suggests. If the observation about the love-romances that rounds off Trim's affair with the young Beguine is a literary-historical view of love, the story behind the tomb of the two lovers (Amandus and Amanda) is both historic and tragic (7:21. 520–22). The encounter with the distracted Maria (a markedly musical episode) is a rapturous and religious view of love (9:24.629–31). The reference to the "poison" creeping into uncle Toby's veins suggests a more cynical perspective hardly different from Walter's. And even the physico-chemical view suggested by Quarles is represented in Tristram's mechanistic account of Toby's fall:

by trotting on too hastily . . . upon an uneasy saddle——worse horse, &c. &c. . . . it had so happened, that the serous part of the blood had got betwixt the two skins, in the nethermost part of my uncle *Toby*——the first shootings of which (as my uncle *Toby* had no experience of love) he had taken for a part of the passion—— till the blister breaking in the one case——and the other remaining——my uncle *Toby* was presently convinced, that his wound was not a skin-deep-wound——but that it had gone to his heart. (8:26.580)

Death, like the contrasting theme of love, is viewed from a variety of conspicuously contrastive points of view, modulated into a still richer variety of keys. Tristram's own attitude toward death (as toward love) shifts with mood and context. His tale of the death of Le Fever is perhaps the most sentimental of the novel's treatments of death, saved only by the abrupt, self-mocking transition at the end, the refusal to "go on" milking the episode for all its pathetic worth (6:6–10.416–26). His treatment of the death of Yorick rivals the story of Le Fever for pathos, but it too is checked by a less serious impulse, and in general its tone, though clearly sentimental, is more convincing (1:12.27–32). His own impending death, however, proves more energizing than debilitating, in a sense more salutary than sorrowful. It is answered not with futility or tears, but with a determination to write more hurriedly still or, as in volume 7, to fly for his life to the Continent, to lead death "a dance he little thinks of" and leave him breathlessly behind. In a sense, the entire seventh volume is an extended variation on the theme of death, but it is only the longest of many.

The richest source of modulated variations on the death theme is the death of Tristram's older brother Bobby. Almost every member of the Shandy household is on hand to register his characteristic and characterizing response. For Toby, Bobby's death (or Walter's oration upon it) is a wellspring of associations with his hobbyhorse, a reminder of warfare and heroic death in battle. For Susannah it is the spur to a mental procession of her mistress's wardrobe, which she covets and might inherit if Elizabeth follows her son. For Obadiah it is a reminder of work to be done: "we shall have a terrible piece of work of it in stubbing the ox-moor." For the coachman it is a sign of the hurry of time and the brevity of life: "He was alive last *Whitson-tide*, said the coachman." And for the foolish scullion it is a cause for selfish satisfaction that it is Bobby and not she who has died: "He is dead! said *Obadiah*,—he is certainly dead!—— So am not I, said the foolish scullion" (5:7.360). But above all it is an opportunity for Walter and Trim, those two very different but equally masterful rhetoricians, to display their eloquence in consecutive, tonally contrasting variations on the theme: "dissimilars solving the same problem." "A curious observer of nature," Tristram remarks, would have given half his fortune "to have heard corporal *Trim* and my father, two orators so contrasted by nature and education, haranguing over the same bier.

My father a man of deep reading——prompt memory——with *Cato*, and *Seneca*, and *Epictetus*, at his fingers ends.——

The corporal——with nothing——to remember——of no deeper reading than his muster-roll——or greater names at his finger's end, than the contents of it.

The one proceeding from period to period, by metaphor and allusion, and striking the fancy as he went along, (as men of wit and fancy do) with the entertainment and pleasantry of his pictures and images.

The other, without wit or antithesis, or point, or turn, this way or that; but leaving the images on one side, and the pictures on the other, going strait forwards as nature could lead him, to the heart. (5:7.359)

The two variations are as different and as revealing as Tristram promises. The corporal's, rich in moving rhetorical questions and eloquently affective gestures, strikes directly on the heart. Walter's, troped by his brother's contrapuntal interjections on military sacrifice and heroism, is a sober stoical treatise made up primarily of improvised divisions on the theme of death:

" 'Tis an inevitable chance——the first statute in *Magnâ Chartâ* ——it is an everlasting act of parliament, my dear brother,——*All must die.*

"If my son could not have died, it had been matter of wonder, ——not that he is dead."

"Monarchs and princes dance in the same ring with us."

"——*To die*, is the great debt and tribute due unto nature: tombs and monuments, which should perpetuate our memories, pay it themselves. (5:3.353)

War is another theme subject to extensive modulation and variation. Unlike love or death, the war theme is limited almost exclusively to two principal voices——Toby's and Trim's. But it is richly developed within those limits. War, as Samuel Monk observes, is viewed as "pure theory, in Toby's studies in ballistics and fortification; as grim reality in the account of Trim's wound or of the flux that attacked the besiegers at the siege of Limerick; as heroic glory in a dozen passages [particularly the extended set piece, "*My uncle* Toby's *apologetical oration* in defence of the profession of arms"]; and nostaligically as remote and unreal in the campaigns on the bowling green." One might add to Monk's perceptive summary that war is also a vehicle for sexual elaboration and innuendo in the many references to the incompletely described battle wound in uncle Toby's groin, and for both comedy and metaphor in the reciprocal "attacks" and "sieges" that comprise the brief and ill-fated amours of Toby and Mrs. Wadman. "Such rich thematic treatment of ideas (and there are others) gives to *Tristram Shandy* a texture that no other novel of the century possesses." [18] The texture, as I hope this discussion makes clear, is the texture of music.

One purpose of the modulation in *Tristram Shandy* may be to illustrate, as almost everything in the novel does, the complexity and fluidity of the mind, its capacity to view ideas and events in a dozen different ways at as many different times. Like Toby, Walter, and the others, Tristram has his own notions about love and death and they are as varied and as changeable as he is. A subject may be viewed, as

Quarles suggests, emotionally, scientifically, religiously, or metaphysically, and the attitude may vary from cynicism to sentimentalism to comedy. It is an awesome demonstration of the multiplicity of individual perception and the complexity and variability of the human mind. There is no one consistent view of the world or experience in *Tristram Shandy*, but multiple views, each exhibiting its own validity; and while it may be possible to step from here to a *Ring and the Book* affirmation of the ultimate relativity of truth, and while Sterne may even encourage that step at times, it is safer to regard perspectivism in *Tristram Shandy* as an illustration not so much of the relativity of truth as its complexity. The views are contrastive, not contradictory, and they are primarily matters of approach and response rather than fact. Sterne is more interested in the multiplexity of truth than its logical status and more concerned with the entrapment of the mind than with the truth of solipsism. But while he may stop short of using the technique of multiple variation to stake out an epistemological claim for the relativity of truth or the impossibility of ever arriving at it, he does use it to take him beyond the portrayal of individual consciousness to a representation of the partiality, multiplicity, and yet validity of the various perspectives we bring to the world. Through modulation, Sterne goes beyond mind to minds and beyond the complexity of consciousness to the complexity of reality itself. Each of us shuts one eye, squints through his own inverted narrow glass, yet somehow manages to glimpse a little piece of what is there.

Modulation is not always a transition from mood to mood or from one perspective to another. It may also mark a shift of subject. Phutatorius's resounding "Zounds!————"

is such a modulation: "One or two who had very nice ears, and could distinguish the expression and mixture of the two tones as plainly as a *third* or a *fifth*, or any other chord in musick——were the most puzzled and perplexed with it ——the *concord* was good in itself——but then 'twas quite out of the key, and no way applicable to the subject started; ——so that with all their knowledge, they could not tell what in the world to make of it" (4:27.318). And similarly, the word *bridge*, meant by Walter as a reference to Tristram's nose but taken by Toby as a reference to his fortifications on the bowling green, functions as a kind of pivot chord (I will resist the temptation to call it a bridge passage) effecting a transition from the themes of birth and noses to that of warfare. Like the pivot chord through which musical modulations occur, the term *bridge* is ambiguous: it can be interpreted as belonging to either key and so serves as a smooth transition by association from one subject or theme to the next. This ambiguity or dual interpretability lies at the root of mental associationism, so it is not surprising that this kind of transition between contrasting subjects—love and war, sex and war, sex and noses, etc.—is quite common in *Tristram Shandy*. But it is only one of an almost inexhaustible variety of transitions Tristram effects between an equally rich variety of contrasting elements.

### Transition and contrast

The musicalization of fiction, writes Quarles, can be achieved in "the changes of moods, the abrupt transitions (Majesty alternating with a joke, for example). . . . Get this into a novel. How? The abrupt transitions are easy enough. All you need is a sufficiency of characters and parallel, contrapuntal plots. While Jones is murdering a wife, Smith is wheeling the perambulator in the park. You alternate the themes." Once again—in the use of transitions and contrast as well as modulation—Sterne anticipates Huxley and surpasses him.

Huxley would capture the abrupt changes of mood in music (majesty alternating with a joke) by alternating themes. Sterne quickly alters mood by shifting theme and subject, but also effects these emotive transitions, as music does, without necessarily shifting themes. And these are only two of the countless kinds of transition Tristram employs. "The digressive style of *Tristram Shandy*," as one writer has pointed out, "makes the transition from volume to volume only a particular instance of the many transitions which are such a feature of the book's narrative structure."[19] We have already seen (in chapter 4) the parallel, contrapuntal plots, complicated by the simultaneity of mental as well as physical phenomena, crossing time zones as well as space. A few strolls, no wife-murders, but very nearly everything else. While Toby taps his pipe against his thumb, we are taken for a ride with Aunt Dinah and the coachman. While Obadiah is off in search of Dr. Slop, uncle Toby is brought from Namur, across Flanders, and into England. While Tristram muses at his desk, uncle Toby whistles "Lillabullero" at the Widow's door. While the adult Tristram enters Lyons with his post chaise in a thousand pieces, young Tristram strolls across the marketplace with his father and uncle and the author sits at his desk in the pavilion on the banks of the Garonne "rhapsodizing all these affairs."

But the rapid transitions may also be explicitly emotive, and may take place within a single dramatic context. There is little majesty in *Tristram Shandy*, but much joy, rapture, frustration, sobriety and pathos, all alternating with each other and "with a joke." The classic instance is the account of the death of Le Fever:

The blood and spirits of *Le Fever*, which were waxing cold and slow within him, and were retreating to their last citadel, the heart,——rallied back,——the film forsook his eyes for a moment,—— he looked up wishfully in my uncle *Toby*'s face,——then cast a look upon his boy,——and that *ligament*, fine as it was,——was never broken.——

Nature instantly ebb'd again,——the film returned to its place, ——the pulse fluttered——stopp'd——went on——throb'd—— stopp'd again——moved——stopp'd——shall I go on?——No. (6:10.426)

This is an extreme case—pathos alternating with and checked by humor—but abrupt transitions from one plane of feeling to another are among the most distinctive marks of a persistently distinctive style. The Latin epigraph to volume 3, taken and slightly altered from *Policraticus* of John of Salisbury, translates: "I do not fear the opinions of the ignorant crowd; nevertheless I pray that they spare my little work, in which it has ever been my purpose to pass from the gay to the serious and from the serious again to the gay."[20] The quotation is appropriate everywhere as Tristram leaps from comedy to rapture, from sobriety to gaiety, from joy to frustration, and from sentiment to irony. Like the modulations, these emotional vacillations and retractions suggest both the complexity of thought and feeling and the equal validity of conflicting perspectives. When Tristram shifts from pathos to comedy as in the story of Le Fever or the distracted Maria (and as Yorick does everywhere in *A Sentimental Journey*), he is not merely toying with us, not merely showing the fickleness of human response, and not necessarily (as Ernest Dilworth suggests)[21] mocking his own sentimentality any more than a musical joke inevitably mocks the majesty that may precede it. He is qualifying points of view, compressing into successive moments of a single experience the testimony of modulation and variation: namely that many even contrasting or seemingly conflicting responses to the same idea or incident are possible and that each has its own validity.

Above all else, however, the rapid transitions, the changes of mood, are images of the fluidity of feeling and the emotive life. Like the German romantic poets of half a century later, Sterne seeks through such transitions "to snatch a grace from music and so to express the subtle nuances of shifting moods and passions."[22] The effort is well grounded not only in music, but in eighteenth-century treatises on musical practice and theory. Since each piece of music is "capable of possessing a mixture of thoughts—pathetic, caressing, gay, sublime,—or light, you must at each bar, so to speak, adopt another passion, and be sad, gay, serious, &c., as these changes are absolutely necessary in music."[23] The similarity between this eighteenth-century instruction to composers and the inscription to volume 3 of *Tristram Shandy* is striking, and the practice had its psychological justification. Musical (and all other) pleasure, wrote Daniel Webb,

is not, as some have imagined, the result of any fixed or permanent condition of the nerves and spirits, but springs from a succession of impressions, and is greatly augmented by sudden or gradual transitions from one kind or strain of vibrations to another. It appears further, that the correspondence between music and passion is most striking in those movements and transitions which in each are productive of the greatest pleasure; consequently the source of pleasure must be in both the same, and the foundation of their union can be no other than a common principle of motion.[24]

The sense of constant motion is also one of the principal sources of pleasure in the reading of Sterne's novel. It is pleasurable in both instances because of a common parallel between medium and observer, because of the correspondence between this fluidity, this perpetual transitiveness, and the movements of feeling and consciousness music and *Tristram Shandy* mirror and express. "It is contrary to the nature of passion," Webb observes, "to rest at any fixed point: ... From the moment that a passion falls within the compass of expression, we cannot even conceive it, much less can we represent it, so as to separate from it the idea of increase or diminution. That action therefore which brings the mind to a full stop cannot be the representative of a mind in motion."[25] Except for the rests, the cadences and codas that have their counterparts in music, there is no such action in *Tristram Shandy*. "I have a great respect for the Shandean dish," wrote Herbert Read; "it has a part in the rhythm of Sterne's periods, which would often avoid anything so abrupt as a full stop!"[26] Tristram's mind is perpetually in motion and as a result everything in his book is in constant flux. Transitions are by way of association in the mind of the author, uncle Toby, or another member of the household. They are sometimes smooth, more often winding and torturous, most often swift and sudden. An entire chapter or group of chapters may play a primarily transitional role, or a mere period, dash, or series of asterisks may do. They are simply upon us, suddenly there, jumping us from plot to digression, from digression to subdigression and back to plot, from narration to direct address to scene, from scene to commentary, document, or interpolated tale, from tale to sermon and sermon to curse. They shift us from present to past and from past to present, more distant past, or future; from character to character, scene to scene, from tale to teller and teller to reader, and, to take us back to Philip Quarles, from theme to theme. Music, Carroll Pratt observes, is "a kaleidoscope of ever-changing tonal configuration,"[27] and if we broaden the concept of "tonal" to include, as in fact it does, emotive and thematic configurations as well, we both broaden our definition of music and emerge with a healthy working description of *Tristram Shandy*.

The pervasive stress on dramatic contrast and transition in *Tristram Shandy* is parallel to if not in fact a product of the music emergent in Sterne's time. The blending of the serious and the comic, bad taste to the early baroque musician, became to Mozart and other composers of the classical sonata, a form of psychological truth and a means of access to the human heart. Tonal drama and thematic contrasts were the essence of the sonata principle. The monothematic "affective" concentration of baroque music gave way to a dynamic style which valued and encouraged the free and deliberate search for contrasting shades of expression.[28] The change was not sudden and unexpected but a gradual evolutionary development distinctly audible in the music of the first half of the eighteenth century. The "galant" symphony, the concerto grosso of Handel, Corelli and Vivaldi, the Italian operas, the oratorios, the music of C.P.E. and Johann Christian (the London) Bach, and the clavier sonatas of Domenico Scarlatti all make effective and pervasive use of dramatic contrast, transition, and surprise. The shift is related to the rise of tonality. Alongside the predominantly unithematic music of the middle baroque grew the newer dualistic form resting on the contrasting properties of the two polar points of tonality, the tonic and the dominant, each associated with its own contrasting theme.[29] But contrasting thematic material was only one aspect of the growing emphasis on contrast in early eighteenth-century music. As in *Tristram Shandy*, it is related to the increasing dramatic and emotive impulse of the period, and it takes a wide variety of forms.

The popular *sonata da chiesa* or church sonata was formed out of pairs of movements, each pair consisting of a slow and quick movement, with further contrasts of time and structure between the quick movements and of key between the slower ones. In the concerto grosso, perhaps the most popular instrumental form of the period, a number of contrastive effects were blended together. In addition to the contrast between its three movements there was the basic contrast between the ritornello for full orchestra and the concertino for solo instruments, which in turn gave rise to further contrasts of dynamics (the forte of the full orchestra versus the more muted sound of the solo parts), and between the plain melody carried by the orchestra and its transformation through solo virtuosity.[30] By far the most important and popular orchestra of the 1750s and sixties was the Mannheim orchestra under the leadership of the Czech violinist and composer, Johann Stamitz. Stamitz characteristically built up the first subject of his galant symphonies out of a number of short, pregnant motives and introduced contrast into the opening subject. He thereby opened the way for the thematic fragmentation and development through contrast of the classical symphony, and earned a strong claim as originator of the contrasted sonata-allegro form itself. But the trademark of the Mannheim orchestra and of the new style was the broad range of feeling and the sudden contrasts in dynamics—a habitual yet surprising alternation between booming fortissimos and barely audible pianissimos for dramatic and emotive effect. Stamitz and other galant composers frequently abused the powers of contrast, but audiences loved it.

Clearly there are similarities between Stamitz's style and Sterne's, but the two composers whose practices most nearly parallel his are C.P.E. Bach (1714–1788) and Domenico Scarlatti (1685–1757). The mark of Bach's music is subjectivity, personalism, and emotivism expressed through sudden dynamic contrasts and pregnant silences, the mixture of dynamism and languid sensibility and the pervasive, often excessive reliance on surprise—anything to frustrate the listener's expectation.[31] His characteristic paradoxes have been described by Basil Lam as "the too-easy surprises of a style where anything may happen," a description ("too easy" most often excepted) hardly less applicable to *Tristram Shandy*. In his use of dramatic contrast, transition, and surprise, Scarlatti, whose music Tristram refers to, is closer still to the author of *Tristram Shandy*. As the son of the great operatic composer Alessandro Scarlatti, Domenico grew up in an operatic atmosphere clearly reflected in his more than 500 short keyboard "exercises" or "sonatas." Here are two descriptions of his style:

The many contrasts in texture, the subtle extensions of his thematic ideas, the intricate figuration—these, it seems, exactly mirror his flexibility and resourcefulness as a player. He was probably the first composer to develop the use of two contrasting themes as a conscious principle of construction, and this alone would make him important in the early history of "sonata". . . .
Outwardly, he is the brilliant executant, the entertainer of the

court. But behind the mask of "impersonality" there is a passion, a savage irony, that mocks and parodies the conventions. His tone is aristocratic, in a way that Mozart would have appreciated; yet such freedom of invention was hardly known outside the framework of the *fantasia*.

Scarlatti's combination of freedom and coherence ... makes the customary description of his style—"half-way between the world of the old polyphony and that of the *galant* era"—seem irrelevant and meaningless.[32]

The first conscious attempt to use contrasting material was made by Domenico Scarlatti (1685–1757). . . . This greatest of harpsichord virtuosi was the composer of over five hundred short keyboard pieces, originally called "exercises" but usually referred to as "sonatas." In the majority of cases this is a misnomer, because while the "sonatas" have a definite exposition section, often with two contrasting themes, followed by a development section, the third part, the recapitulation, is too rudimentary to be considered a reprise in the sonata manner. The brevity of this treatment would give the impression of a simple binary form were it not for the capricious technique of pianistic writing, jumping from polyphony to homophony and thereby effectively enhancing the contrasting element, less equivocally indicated in melody and rhythm.

The radiant and piquant melody, the colorful and exuberant vivacity, the sudden changes from frivolous playfulness to powerful dramatic accents betray the operatic influence.[33]

The parallels between Scarlatti and Sterne—largely, but by no means exclusively in terms of contrast and transition —are distinct, plentiful, and fundamental: flexibility and resourcefulness; brilliant execution and courtly entertainment masking irony and the mockery of convention; the combination of coherence and freedom of invention; the structural use of contrastive thematic material; the capricious technique emphasizing the contrasts between polyphony and homophony, melody and rhythm; the sudden shifts from the frivolous to the dramatic and profound. And enclosing it all, a form hovering between binary and sonata or three-part form and consisting, as does *Tristram Shandy*, of an exposition, a development section, and a brief and underdeveloped recapitulation. This last parallel takes us to the last aspect of the musical treatment of themes in *Tristram Shandy:* closure by means of a rudimentary recapitulation of basic themes.

## *Recapitulation*

Although all things, *Tristram Shandy* included, come to an end, there is an aura of the interminable about this novel. Everything, it seems, leads to everything else; everything ramifies and expands—by analogy, double entendre, causal relation, verbal or thematic association. "Sterne's development of his various themes never creates in his reader a sense of either immanent or imminent cessation; instead, the atmosphere is charged with a sense of virtually infinite and inscrutable extension, aborted only by the possibility of death."[34] It is precisely this widening expansiveness that puts his project, at least ostensibly, beyond Tristram's own reach. Nothing, he finds—neither sentences nor paragraphs, chapters nor volumes, plot nor digression, and least of all his history—is quite so simple to round off as the works of other writers seem to suggest.

Could a historiographer drive on his history, as a muleteer drives on his mule,——straight forward;——for instance, from *Rome* all the way to *Loretto*, without ever once turning his head aside either to the right hand or to the left,——he might venture to foretell you to an hour when he should get to his journey's end;—— but the thing is, morally speaking, impossible: For, if he is a man of the least spirit, he will have fifty deviations from a straight line

to make with this or that party as he goes along, which he can no
ways avoid. . . .

  In short, there is no end of it. (1:14.36–37)

Instead of narrowing in toward climax and closure, everything continually expands before Tristram like a road
lengthening before a breathless runner. One day in his life
is a year in the recounting and three hundred and sixty-five
more such days are added to the task. To this, Sisyphus has a
sinecure, and E. M. Forster, though he did not know it,
had his model.

  What Forster was looking for in fiction was a way to
combine pattern with life, to achieve not rigid form but a
sense of overall structure or "rhythm" without sacrificing
or compromising the infinite multifariousness that life provides. "Human beings," says Forster,

have their great chance in the novel. They say to the novelist: "Recreate us if you like, but we must come in," and the novelist's
problem, as we have seen all along, is to give them a good run and
to achieve something else at the same time. Whither shall he
turn? not indeed for help but for analogy. Music, though it does not
employ human beings, though it is governed by intricate laws,
nevertheless does offer in its final expression a type of beauty
which fiction might achieve in its own way. Expansion. That is
the idea the novelist must cling to. Not completion. Not rounding
off but opening out.[35]

Forster did not see it. To him *Tristram Shandy* was a novel
of "Fantasy" ruled by a god whose name was Muddle. But
his description of the novel of expansion, of the fiction that,
like music, continually opens out, is an accurate and instructive account of the basic procedural principle governing the
development of *Tristram Shandy*.

  Musical expansion, however, is not endless expansion,
and though Tristram warns us that "there is no end of it,"

inevitably there is. Almost by definition, statement and development in music demand a rounding off, a recapitulation of the principal theme or themes. Recapitulation is all but indispensable to musical form, "as inveterate," said D. F. Tovey, "as symmetry is in architecture."[36] Because literature is by nature referential, it is characteristically linear in structure—or was until the twentieth-century breakdown of belief in the causal and logical beginning, middle, and end structure of reality inherited from Aristotle. Where referentialism dictates development, repetition and return are deviations from the norm; taken to excess, they produce grievous monotony. Music, on the other hand, is characteristically circular. Because it is so remote from any world outside its own, its sense of completeness cannot come from anything but a further development of its own materials, usually in the form of a climactic recapitulation of its themes. To an unusual degree the same is true of Sterne's novel. In order to make its central referential point about the mind of its author, *Tristram Shandy* (like a musical composition) must attend primarily to the internal processes and intrinsic relationships that mirror the habits of that mind. Like music, *Tristram Shandy* is in this sense remarkably introverted: with the tail-in-the-mouth form of a musical composition it circles back on itself and ends with a recapitulation of major themes.[37]

Since *Tristram Shandy* is a work of fiction, not a piece of music, it is rich in rational and referential content, and we can hardly expect an exact or near exact culminative return of the opening as was conventional in many popular eighteenth-century musical forms. There is no identical recapitulation in *Tristram Shandy*. But it is a testimony to the essential musicality of the novel, to the musical world it creates and the musical expectations it generates, that we would be shocked not at all if the opening chapters were to reappear verbatim at the end. We would acknowledge, I think, that this was indeed one of the possible ways to end this seemingly unendable book. There is no identical return at the end, but there is something equally appropriate to *Tristram Shandy* and equally natural to music: a modified and abbreviated recapitulation of the main, chiefly the expository themes.

Recapitulation is not unique to the final chapter or volume of the novel. Periodic and compressed reiterations of theme or event, summary reminders of where we have been, what territory we have covered and how we have traveled it are among the principal supports that save the swaying structure from collapse. "My Father's Lamentation" in chapter 19 of the fourth volume is a concise recounting of the accidents that bent and doomed his star-crossed son: his conception, delivery, and naming. Volume 6 opens with an invitation to a backward glance:

We'll not stop two moments, my dear Sir,——only, as we have got thro' these five volumes, (do, Sir, sit down upon a set——they are better than nothing) let us just look back upon the country we have pass'd through.——
——What a wilderness has it been! and what a mercy that we have not both of us been lost, or devoured by wild beasts in it. (6:1.408)

The beginning of the second major division or movement of the novel midway through the sixth volume is preceded by a summary account of those who, in the act of moving on, are left behind, and in what condition. This same volume ends with diagrams of the digressive structure of the preceding installments, a self-congratulatory description of the

more disciplined linearity of volume 6, and a quickly re-
tracted suggestion that perhaps from here on out the road
may narrow to a perfectly straight line. As in music, summary repetition is not merely a terminative device. In various abbreviated forms it appears periodically and for the
same reason: to strengthen internal coherence, consummate
the development of a given segment and round it off, and to
reinforce the always threatened sense of recognition and
connectedness essential to meaning. In the final volume,
however, and particularly in its final chapters, repetition
and restatement take the fuller and more climactic form of
final recapitulation.

For one thing, there is an increased number of tacit or
overt reminders of what has gone before, dramatic and
thematic connectives linking the concluding volume with
what has brought us so drunkenly and belatedly to it. In
the first chapter of volume 9 Tristram takes us back to the
first pages of the novel with a reminder of his mother's
lack of prurience, the circumstances of his begetting, and the
consequences of both:

A temperate current of blood ran orderly through her veins in all
months of the year, and in all critical moments both of the day and
night alike; nor did she superinduce the least heat into her humours
from the manual effervescencies of devotional tracts, which having
little or no meaning in them, nature is oft times obliged to find
one——And as for my father's example! 'twas so far from being
either aiding or abetting thereunto, that 'twas the whole business
of his life to keep all fancies of that kind out of her head——Nature had done her part, to have spared him this trouble; and what
was not a little inconsistent, my father knew it——And here am
I sitting, this 12th day of *August*, 1766, in a purple jerkin and
yellow pair of slippers, without either wig or cap on, a most tragi-
comical completion of his prediction, "That I should neither think,
nor act like any other man's child, upon that very account."
(9:1.600)

A few pages later, we find his parents walking arm in arm "till they had got to the fatal angle of the old garden wall, where Doctor *Slop* was overthrown by *Obadiah* on the coach-horse" (on his way to deliver Tristram back in volume 2). Eavesdropping on uncle Toby and Widow Wadman, they speculate on the impending marriage and on the begetting and bearing of a child (9:11.612–14). Their conversation triggers an association in Walter's mind with his own monthly obligations to sex and procreation, and the emergence of Yorick's congregation from church, combined with his wife's assurance that "it was a sacrament day" inform him that this is indeed the first Sunday of the month, a date of fatal import to the narrator and another sudden projection back to the first chapter of the book. Mrs. Wadman's persistent probes into the exact whereabouts and extent of Toby's groin injury remind Tristram of an illustratively parallel tale in Slawkenbergius, which takes us back to volume 4 and to the related themes of sex and impotence. And finally, while pondering how to get on with his story of Toby and the widow, Tristram is transported back to his journey through France (volume 7) to the moment when the thought of his uncle's amours put him into sympathetic harmony with poor Maria.[38]

But all this—this sense of a final recapitulatory gathering —comes to a head (or tail) in the final chapter of the book. To begin with, except for Mrs. Wadman, an outsider now unwelcome, and Tristram himself, who by this time has managed to get himself unborn again, the final scene brings together for the first and only time every major character in the novel. Walter and Mrs. Shandy, Toby and Trim, Yorick, Susannah, Dr. Slop and Obadiah are all there—gathered, it seems, in ironic parting deference to convention. More important still, and more conspicuous, is the final restatement of most of the major themes introduced in the expositional first chapter and developed throughout the work.

Discovering at last the real source of Mrs. Wadman's persistent queries into the condition of his groin (sex and crossed communication) and his "siege" of the widow's "fort" thus ending in defeat for both (war), uncle Toby has come to pay his brother a visit. Walter, however, already knows what Toby plans to tell him, and when Toby arrives he is well along in a learned and cynical diatribe contrasting the sullying nature of the organs and act of procreation (conception, sex, and paradoxical hypotheses) with the dignity and glory of the instruments and methods of destruction (warfare again). Walter has little taste for sex—hence the restriction to first Sundays—his wife still less—hence the question, and the result of their distaste, part of which is explained by Walter's hypothesis, is that "child of decrepitude! interruption! mistake! and discontent" (carelessness and misfortune) and the autobiography one might expect from such a product. As Booth points out, in his lament that generation must take place under such sordid conditions, it is as though Walter were anticipating the portentous opening scene and rebuking his wife in advance for her fateful question about the clock.[39]

Characteristically, Walter is not allowed to finish formulating his hypothesis. As he prepares to go on with it, as Toby prepares to intercede and as Yorick rises to batter it to pieces, Obadiah bursts into the room with a complaint about the Shandy bull "which cried out for an immediate hearing." Obadiah's interruption, the closing act of the novel, marks a fitting end, balancing the interruption that begins the book and Tristram's life and duplicating the pervasive interruptive procedure of the narrative. Here Walter is discoursing on procreation, there he was working at it. But something breaks in to interrupt him at both ends, just as Tristram, "child of interruption," laboring at his own special act of creation, is interfered with everywhere between by a thousand things which break in upon his mind and likewise cry out for an immediate hearing. Then, too, as with Tristram's burglars, dressed in black and working in darkness, Obadiah's interruption bears a close resemblance to what it bursts in on. As with most of these digressions, the relationship is thematic: Obadiah interrupts Walter's discourse upon begetting with a complaint about the impotence of the Shandy bull. Once again we are thrown back to the expository and pervasive themes of conception, birth, impotence, and sterility. The closing interruptive question about the bull is not only a dramatic image of a pervasive narrative technique traceable to the opening question about the clock, but a culminative iteration of the theme of sterility and impotence that touches and engulfs uncle Toby (the injury to his groin and the sterile battles on the bowling green), Walter (his futile efforts to write his *Tristra-pædia* or to alter his son's fortune), and above all Tristram, both as wounded child and as drowning narrator. This closing theme, like the procedural vehicle that carries it and like virtually all else in the novel, is launched in the exposition —in the enfeebled animal spirits transfused from futile father to misbegotten son. "In short," as Booth observes, "we have a thematic return which seems deliberate, since no other chapter in the whole work resembles so completely the first five chapters of Volume I" as do the last.[40] And no other incident, one might add, resembles so completely the one that begins the novel as the one that brings it to an end.

Mrs. Shandy, whose question begins it all, ends it with another query:

> L—d! said my mother, what is all this story about?——
> A COCK and a BULL, said *Yorick*——And one of the best of its kind, I ever heard. (9:33.647)

Coming at the very end of the book, the *all* in Mrs. Shandy's question, as one reader his suggested,[41] seems to refer to the entire novel—we have been asking this question all along —as does the answer. A cock and bull story is a bawdy joke, but it is also a "long rambling story; or a concocted, incredible story," and since the immediate referent, Walter's declamation on begetting, is neither, Sterne would seem to have intended his final sentence as a summary comic judgment on the entire book. "It was common," as Booth points out, "for earlier facetious writers to call their entire books 'cock-and-bull stories' " and Sterne, "who knew many of these works well, could not but have had this meaning in mind when he wrote that final line."[42] This is a persuasive argument for the contention that Sterne did in fact complete *Tristram Shandy*, and while that is at the same time relevant to my own argument for the conclusion as musical recapitulation, it is equally pertinent and interesting from another, related, point of view. Sterne ended—and very likely intended to end—his book with Yorick's punning observation about a cock and a bull. But by ending it on a pun, a puzzling joke, a chord that is both culminative and pivotal, he ends this open-ended, continuously expansive novel in the only really appropriate way: with an end that, like the ending of Gide's fugal *The Counterfeiters*, implies a new beginning.

Gide, like Sterne before him, viewed the novel as a vehicle for the discussion and representation of man's interminable striving and sacrificed the conventional well-made plot to the inconclusive fullness of life itself. "I invent the character of a novelist," writes Edouard, "whom I make my central figure; and the subject of the book, if you must have one, is just that very struggle between what reality offers him and what he himself desires to make of it. . . . It's essentially out of the question for a book of this kind to have a plan."[43] Originally he had hoped to include everything, all of life in his book, but when that proves (not surprisingly) impossible he hits upon the compensatory device of the ending that does not put an end. Watching the youngest son of the Profitendieu family, Edouard muses provocatively: "I should like to know Caloub," a last line that implies a new beginning. Like *Tristram Shandy*, *The Counterfeiters* is a novel about the writing of a novel, a work characterized by inconclusiveness, nonclosure, and constant rebeginning and with its own ultimate interminability structured into its conception. The open-ended conclusion is Gide's compromise with possibility and at the same time, as Fowlie observes, the demonstration that the novel can, in part at least, imitate the art of the fugue, can be as inconclusive, as incongruous, and as surprising as life itself.

Sterne's ending is similar, similarly musical and for similar reasons. The conclusion of *Tristram Shandy*, like that of *The Counterfeiters* and like some of the earlier and more restricted forms of musical recapitulation, is at the same time a rounding off and an opening out. As in music and particularly the musical scale that is its primary resource, we must come back to where we began, but every return is at the same time at least potentially a possible point of departure. It is an end and yet not an end, or not necessarily. The notion

of beginning, middle, and unmistakable end follows from
the Aristotelian conception of unified action (which in turn
assumes an orderly and rational, i.e. causal, universe) and
in fact heavily depends on it. But for Sterne, as for Gide,
Joyce, Proust, and most other musical novelists, reality is
principally interior, hence less rationally ordered. And like
them, Sterne worked to break away not only from the conventions of logical progression, but from the concomitant
and equally artificial convention of unified action where
every event is contributory and subordinate to a single encompassing action—Tom Jones's reconciliation and reunion
with Sophia Western and Squire Allworthy, for example.
In its place he offered the novel of multiple action on a
crowded and confused mental landscape. One consequence
of this revolution is that in place of the traditional beginning, middle, and end, we have a structure strongly reminiscent of, if not consciously modeled on, the musical pattern
of exposition, development, and return. There is no single
plot chronologically developed. Instead there are plots, incidents, set pieces, and opinions permeated and connected
by a number of major themes that are introduced in the
opening chapter, fragmented, combined, modulated, varied,
and woven to form what follows, and cumulatively reca-
pitulated at the end. A second consequence is the special
open-endedness of that ending. In a fictive organism com-
prised not merely of several plots but of dozens, and where
logical and chronological order are subordinated to complex
thematic interplay, the traditional ending, the conclusion
that neatly wraps things up, that literally concludes and
terminates the ongoing action, is not only unlikely but for-
biddingly cumbersome and inevitably strained. It is tying
a hundred knots on the package and in the process squashing

the contents and obscuring the address. It is all very neat no doubt and quite secure, but it misses the point—the attempt to present life as it flows in all its intractable and irresolvable multiplicity through the mind. Actions do not end so well as they are famed to do. Conclusion, if Tristram is to adhere to his truth, must be the mirror of exposition and development in this sense too: it must cling to Forster's idea of musical expansion. Not completion. Not rounding off but opening out. Ending the novel is, in an important sense, no different from beginning or developing it. Here too the meeting ground of life and art, whose reconciliation Tristram, like Edouard and Philip Quarles, puzzled over, lies, as Forster said it might, in music: in the restatement or return that is in one sense a conclusion but at the same time an open-ended invitation to further expansion, the tonic that is the dominant of another familiar key.

# 5

## Concentricity: Wheels within Wheels

---

### *The Musical Parts*

So far we have dealt mainly with forms, patterns, and techniques that permeate and govern the entire novel. Now I want to move in closer and focus on the interior design. What we find as we close in are wheels spinning within wheels, the shapes, features, and movements of the whole mirrored concentrically, as in music, on a diminishing scale. We find too that as we work our way toward the teeth and screws of the novel—through volume, sequence, and chapter down to utterance, word, and intonation—musicality grows increasingly explicit. "The Symphonic novel," wrote Paul Emile Cadilhac, "will create a musical atmosphere by the use of images, comparisons, and words borrowed from the musical vocabulary."[1] In these terms Sterne's novel is "symphonic."[2] Music metaphors proliferate in *Tristram Shandy*, fusing under sheer numerical weight into a cohesive family of references, a pervasive "music motif" reinforcing an already strong feeling that the book is in many ways analogous—in quality, structure, and effect—to a musical composition.

The largest definable component of the novel identified with music is one of its nine volumes, volume 7. Tristram calls it a dance.[3] At the outset, Tristram gave fair warning about the odd reading experience we were in for when he compared his habitual narrative meanderings to a dance. An author, he explained, never knows "what lets and confounded hinderances he is to meet with in his way,——or what a dance he may be led, by one excursion or another, before all is over" (1:14.36).[4] The metaphor is appropriate to the patterned digressiveness of *Tristram Shandy* in general. But the seventh volume is a kind of crystallization, an epitome of the vagrant whole, and the dance metaphor is more clearly applicable there, and more frequently applied. Literally an excursion through continental Europe and structurally the longest of all digressions from the plot, it is, by the narrator's own account, a dance within a dance.

The volume deals almost entirely with Tristram-as-adult, a sickly man in flight from death on a galloping grand tour of Europe. As Tristram describes it, "I will lead him a dance he little thinks of—for I will gallop, quoth I, without looking once behind me to the banks of the *Garonne*; and if I hear him clattering at my heels——I'll scamper away to mount *Vesuvius*——from thence to *Joppa*, and from *Joppa* to the world's end, where, if he follows me, I pray God he may break his neck" (7:1.480).

This is no idle metaphor. The galloping tour is in effect a sequence of steps in a rollicking gigue, as Tristram flees from inn to inn and town to town, springs into his chaise and out again and fairly leaps from Calais to Boulogne, from Boulogne to Montreuil:

*de Montreuil à Nampont - poste et demi*
*de Nampont à Bernay - - - poste*
*de Bernay à Nouvion - - - poste*
*de Nouvion à Abbeville poste.*

.      .      .

Hollo! Ho!——the whole world's asleep!——bring out the horses ——grease the wheels——tie on the mail——and drive a nail into that moulding——I'll not lose a moment——. (7:10.491; 7:13. 493)

"We danced it along," writes Tristram, "to *Ailly au cloch-ers*, famed in days of yore for the finest chimes in the world." (7:15.495). The dance metaphor, then, has a double re-ferent. Volume 7 is a "dance" first in the established meta-phorical sense of extended digression, an excursion from the story, and second, in that the journey itself takes on some-thing of the character of a dance—a dance, as Tristram describes it, not of death but away from it.[5]

Not all the dancing on Tristram's tour is implicit or metaphorical. In Paris, for example, he happens upon a may-pole dance (a dance within a dance—volume 7—within a dance—the entire digressive novel): "Tantarra-ra-tan-tivi ——the whole world was going out a May-poling—— frisking here——capering there." (7:38.530). He is so charmed by the dance that he begins to consider the possi-bilities and joys of importing it to England. If the French were to send them maypoles, he reflects, "The women would set them up; and when they had done, they would dance round them (and the men for company) till they were all blind" (7:38.531). By the end of the journey, Tristram is rejuvenated. He has left Death gasping for air and no longer need confine his joy to speculations. When he comes upon Nanette and her joyous company all the stops are out. A youth

struck the note upon the tabourin——his pipe followed, and off we bounded. . . .
　The sister of the youth who had stolen her voice from heaven, sung alternately with her brother——'twas a *Gascoigne* roundelay." (7:43.538)

Their gaiety is infectious, and Tristram would like nothing more than to end his days among them, to sit down "in the lap of content here——and dance, and sing, and say his prayers, and go to heaven with this nut brown maid" (7:43. 538). But Tristram prefers imagined Eden to the real but more precarious pleasures of the fallen world, and when she threatens his idyll with a seductive gesture, the traveller retreats. He takes his dance out of its literal context and, musical to the end, returns to his original metaphor:

> Then 'tis time to dance off, quoth I; so changing only partners and tunes, I danced it away from *Lunel* to *Montpellier*——from thence to *Pesçnas, Beziers*——I danced it along through *Narbonne, Carcasson*, and *Castle Naudairy*, till at last I danced myself into *Perdrillo*'s pavillion, where pulling a paper of black lines, that I might go on straight forwards, without digression or parenthesis, in my uncle *Toby's* amours——
>
>     I begun thus—— (7:43.538)

This last passage both restores the dance to its original status in volume 7 as a metaphor for Tristram's heady flight from death and at the same time polishes the earlier link between dances and narrative digressions. The whole of this volume, then, is analogous to a dance in the rhythmic scurrying of the author, in the complementary rhythms of the prose, and, as the longest digression in the book, in structural terms as well: it is the "dance [an author] may be led by one excursion or another, before all is over." All the multiple implications are continued into volume 8. Tristram has vowed to carry on in a straight line without further digression. But nature is uncooperative. The whole dance-like journey from which he has just returned (the metaphoric physical dance), most particularly perhaps the dance with Nanette (the literal dance), has inflamed his imagination and made further mental excursions (the metaphoric narrative—dances) unavoidable:

> But softly——for in these sportive plains, and under this genial sun, where at this instant all flesh is running out piping, fiddling, and dancing to the vintage, and every step that's taken, the judgment is surprised by the imagination, I defy, notwithstanding all that has been said upon *straight lines* in sundry pages of my book ——I defy the best cabbage planter that ever existed, whether he plants backwards or forwards, it makes little difference in the account . . . I defy him to go on coolly, critically, and canonically, planting his cabbages one by one, in straight lines, and stoical distances, especially if slits in petticoats are unsew'd up [as Nanette's was]——without ever and anon straddling out, or sidling into some bastardly digression. (8:1.539)

In volume 7 Sterne has dropped a stone in the middle of a pond. Circles ripple within circles; interior patterns echo larger ones which in turn are echoes of the whole. The Gascoigne roundelay is a dance within a dance away from death within an excursive dance away from the plot of a pervasively excursive, hence dance-like, work of fiction. And because of the special nature of the author, his peculiar sensibilities and susceptibilities, each circle radiates the one beyond; the first dance demands and guarantees the last.

Volume 7 is the largest definable unit of *Tristram Shandy* identified by a music metaphor, but only the largest. On a smaller scale the novel reverberates with such analogies. One of the most interesting is subordinate to a broader stage metaphor but rises out of its secondary role like an orchestra out of the pit to steal our attention from the stage and fix it. It is the strange musical interlude that makes up the entire fifteenth chapter of volume 5, the tuning up between the acts.

> Had this volume been a farce, which, unless every one's life and opinions are to be looked upon as a farce as well as mine, I see no

reason to suppose—the last chapter, Sir, had finished the first act of it, and then this chapter must have set off thus.

Ptr..r..r..ing——twing——twang——prut——trut——'tis a cursed bad fiddle.—— Do you know whether my fiddle's in tune or no?——trut..prut..——They should be *fifths.*——'Tis wickedly strung——tr...a.e.i.o.u.-twang.——The bridge is a mile too high, and the sound-post absolutely down,——else——trut . . prut—— hark! 'tis not so bad a tone.——Diddle diddle, diddle diddle, diddle diddle, dum. (5:15.371)[6]

The chapter begins as a mere comic interlude, a kind of musical joke, but before it ends, Sterne has transformed it into another member of a large family of literary homonculi, miniscule interior images of the whole. "O! there is [cries the violinist]——whom I could sit and hear whole days,——whose talents lie in making what he fiddles to be felt,——who inspires me with his joys and hopes, and puts the most hidden springs of my heart into motion" (5:15.372). This sudden shift from the frivolous, chaotic, and absurd ("Diddle diddle, diddle diddle, diddle diddle ——hum——dum——drum . . . ——trut-prut,——prut-trut.") to feeling and the borders of sentimentality is a transition within a transition and a microcosm of Sterne's consistent purpose: to mix the serious with the gay, the comic with the sober and sentimental, and to establish through and in the midst of frivolity and jest affective rapport and emotive communication. Like the string player's, Tristram's aim, repeated wish, and undeniable achievement is to make what he fiddles rise out of the comic and chaotic "to be felt."

Volumes are dance movements; chapters are musical interludes; and stories, as noted in the previous chapter, must be told in their appropriate keys. Sermons too must be read and evaluated as musical compositions. Yorick, Sterne's alter ego in *Tristram Shandy*, narrator of *A Sentimental Journey*, and the alleged author of Sterne's *Sermons*, took a musical view of his homilies. He marked some of them *lentamente*, some *tenutè*, some *grave*, others *adagio*, and so forth. Assuming for the moment the unfamiliar role of musical ingenue, Tristram feigns mystification. What such notations might mean

> as applied to theological compositions, and with which he has characterized some of these sermons, I dare not venture to guess.———— I am more puzzled still upon finding *a l'octava alta!* upon one;———— *Con strepito* upon the back of another;————*Siciliana* upon a third; ————*Alla capella* upon a fourth;————*Con l'arco* upon this;———— *Senza l'arco* upon that.————All I know is, that they are musical terms, and have a meaning;————and as he was a musical man, I will make no doubt, but that by some quaint application of such metaphors to the compositions in hand, they impressed very distinct ideas of their several characters upon his fancy,————whatever they may do upon that of others. (6:11.428)

But that is by no means all he knows. He knows very well what it means to read a sermon musically and to apply such "quaint metaphors" to a composition, whether it be a sermon, a novel, or any other. Earlier on, he had approached a different sermon very much as though it were a piece of music and, as such, another in the chain of duplicating echoes of his own creative effort. Homenas's sermon proves Tristram's point about the primacy of internal harmony in any composition.

> I'm to preach at court next Sunday, said *Homenas*————run over my notes————so I humm'd over doctor *Homenas*'s notes————the modulation's very well————'twill do, *Homenas*, if it holds on at this rate ———— so on I humm'd————and a tolerable tune I thought it was; and to this hour, may it please your reverences, had never found out how low, how flat, how spiritless and jejune it was, but that all of a sudden, up started an air in the middle of it, so fine, so rich, so

heavenly——it carried my soul up with it into the other world; now had I, (as *Montaigne* complained in a parallel accident)—— had I found the declivity easy, or the ascent accessible——certes I had been outwitted——Your notes, *Homenas*, I should have said, are good notes,——but it was so perpendicular a precipice——so wholly cut off from the rest of the work, that by the first note I humm'd, I found myself flying into the other world, and from thence discovered the vale from whence I came, so deep, so low, and dismal, that I shall never have the heart to descend into it again. (4:25.315–16)

If writing a book is like humming a tune, so is writing—or reading—a sermon. The main effort in both is the maintenance of "the just proportions and harmony of the whole." Homenas's glorious "air," like Tristram's own transcendent description of Uncle Toby's cavalcade, must be deleted—not despite its conspicuous superiority to the rest, but because of it. Nothing, not even inspiration, supersedes harmony.

---

## Mirrors of the Incompletable

Each segment of *Tristram Shandy* discussed in this chapter so far (and many that remain to be discussed) reflects the image of still another distinctly musical characteristic of the novel. Each of the parts is a synecdochic repetition of other parts or a microcosm of the whole. *Tristram Shandy*, in other words, like a piece of music, is marked by a kind of concentric involution, a structure—to change the shape of the metaphor—like that of a Chinese box. The novel's multilevel parallelisms have two main sources. Like each other and like the whole of *Tristram Shandy*, each of these segments is in some significant sense musical. In fact, the music motif (the family of music references) is itself doubly musical since by its very nature it is one of the main contributors to the concentricity of the novel. Music metaphors, analogues and references appear in every stratum of the novel, impressing each part with the musical imprint of the whole. But the synecdochic relationship of part to whole is more than a matter of common musicality. For each part also says something else about the novel as a comprehensive unity, and something different. Each mirrors the room from its own special angle.

Tristram regards all of his digressions as mental excursions and as figurative dances of the intellect and imagination. And volume 7, longest of all his digressions, is the crystallization of this total view. In substance it is a physical excursion, in formal terms a narrative one, and in the manner and style of presentation as well as in Tristram's own metaphoric description it is a dance. If volume 7 is in effect the epitomic digression, a microcosm of the impulsive, diversionary whole, the musician's admiring tribute to the fiddler is a comment on Sterne's own godlike effort to bring affective harmony out of chaos. Homenas's sermon is yet another instance of the large writ small, embodying the same preeminent commitment to internal harmony as *Tristram Shandy*. But perhaps the most strikingly mirrorlike microcosms of the whole are the narratives within the narrative—particularly Trim's story of the king of Bohemia—and Walter Shandy's *Tristra-pædia*, the book within the book.

Walter's *Tristra-pædia*, the comprehensive system of education collected for his son, shares the character and fate of *Tristram Shandy*. Like his son's autobiography, it is an encyclopedic combination of original thought and obscure transmogrified erudition, a collection of its author's "scattered thoughts, counsels, and notions . . . spun . . . every thread of it, out of his own brain,——or reeled and cross-twisted what all other spinners and spinsters had spun before him" (5:16.372–73). Like the book, the *Tristra-pædia* is a machine, an "engine" that evolves a volatile, ever-expanding universe of possibility out of grains of verbal sand. Out of a single subject—a white bear—and a single process—conjugation through the system of auxiliary verbs—Walter generates a world:[7]

A WHITE BEAR! Very well. Have I ever seen one? Might I ever have seen one? Am I ever to see one? Ought I ever to have seen one? Or can I ever see one?

Would I had seen a white bear! (for how can I imagine it?)

If I should see a white bear, what should I say? If I should never see a white bear, what then?

If I never have, can, must or shall see a white bear alive; have I ever seen the skin of one? Did I ever see one painted?—described? Have I never dreamed of one?

Did my father, mother, uncle, aunt, brothers or sisters, ever see a white bear? What would they give? How would they behave? How would the white bear have behaved? Is he wild? Tame? Terrible? Rough? Smooth?

——Is the white bear worth seeing?——

——Is there no sin in it?——

Is it better than a BLACK ONE? (5:43.406–7)

As in music, any subject will do. Walter has his bear, Tristram his themes and incidents—love and death, his birth and delivery, mind and body, his naming and accident. Walter "danced his white bear back and forth through half a dozen pages" (6:2.409); Tristram dances his material back and forth through several hundred. But basically the procedures are the same: repetition, complex variation, and continuous expansion; and in both the end result is the splintering of poor Tristram's mind:

every word, *Yorick*, by this means, you see, is converted into a thesis or an hypothesis;———every thesis and hypothesis have an offspring of propositions;———and each proposition has its own consequences and conclusions; every one of which leads the mind on again, into fresh tracks of enquiries and doubtings.———The force of this engine, added my father, is incredible, in opening a child's head.———'Tis enough, brother *Shandy*, cried my uncle *Toby*, to burst it into a thousand splinters. (6:2.409)

Like Tristram, Walter is plagued by an over-fertile, non-selective imagination: "from the very moment he took pen in hand———all the devils in hell broke out of their holes to cajole him. . . . [E]very thought, first and last, was captious" and the business of writing became "not so much a state of *composition*, as a state of *warfare*" (5:16.374). Walter is primarily a defensive warrior and defeats his own book with an impenetrable Maginot line of rigid judicious resistance. Tristram tries to hold out against the multiple assaults of an insistent memory and imagination, but ultimately adopts a kind of Moscow-winter defense absorbing all comers, reducing itself to rubble but, unlike Walter in this at least, winning a kind of victory through self-destruction. Tristram lets too much in, Walter too little. But both are engaged in an overambitious and progressively more hopeless battle with time. At the end of a year's writing Tristram has barely got through the first day of his life. After three years of indefatigable labor Walter has scarce completed one-half of his undertaking. And what is worse, Tristram lives not only a great deal faster than *he* writes; he lives too fast for his father's enterprise as well. The disparity between real and writing time is the bane of the *Tristra-pædia* no less than of *Tristram Shandy* (which is itself, in fact, a kind of Tristra-pædia): Walter "advanced so very slow with his work, and I began to live and get forwards at such a rate" that Walter, like his seed, falls farther and farther behind his objective. "By the very delay, the first part of the work, upon which my father had spent the most of his pains, was rendered entirely useless,——every day a page or two became of no consequence" (5:16.375). Tristram's concluding lament over his father's effort could serve as an inscription to his own enterprise, and, by implication, as an epitaph on the grave of all human ambition: "Certainly it was ordained as a scourge upon the pride of human wisdom, That the wisest of us all, should thus outwit ourselves, and eternally forego our purposes in the intemperate act of pursuing them" (5:16.375).

Trim's untellable tale of the king of Bohemia and his seven castles is another replica of Tristram's narrative impotence, if anything more imitative still of the strange encompassing design and of the methods—many of them musical—that account for the seeming madness. Trim's story is a verbal counterpart of Tristram's own, and like the *Tristra-pædia* it replicates both the special nature of *Tristram Shandy*—in this case more procedural than substantive—and its fate. If Tristram modulates from subject to subject, mood to mood, and theme to theme, Trim hems twice "to find in what key his story would best go, and best suit his master's humour." If Tristram insists on his right to "tell his story in his own way" and embellishes it with the digressions that are the soul of his work, uncle Toby invites Trim to "ornament [his] . . . after thy own fashion" and proceeds to ornament it himself with digressions that become virtually the only soul or substance Trim's upstaged monologue ever acquires. The basic structure of the sequence is statement, departure, and return. Trim announces his title, begins his story in the naive hope of simply telling it from beginning to end, is repeatedly interrupted by uncle

Toby's digressive intrusions, and returns, insistently if less optimistically, to his title and the continuation of his tale. Toby's intrusions, like many of Tristram's into his own tale, begin with associative leaps, requests for clarification, or troped commentary, then develop into lengthly digressive variations on the stated theme (geography and chronology in this case), and ultimately lead to still more distantly related variations on other themes (Trim on love). The segment, like the book, assumes the character of a contrapuntal alternation of voices, sometimes rapid, sometimes more leisurely, each voice related to the other but basically independent, pursuing its own private themes and variations. And in the end it comes to much the same inconclusive halt as the work that contains it. By this time Trim has drifted (as Tristram will) long years from the story he began. He has come, in fact, to the tastiest morsel in his own narrative pantry, the amours not of uncle Toby and Widow Wadman, but of a younger Trim and the fair Beguine. Trim, like Toby, has been wounded in the war, and the Beguine, like the Widow, takes a provocative interest in the soldier's groin. As her strokes move and lengthen from the wounded knee,

at length, by two or three strokes longer than the rest——my passion rose to the highest pitch——I seized her hand——

——And then, thou clapped'st it to thy lips, *Trim*, said my uncle *Toby*——and madest a speech.

Whether the corporal's amour terminated precisely in the way my uncle *Toby* described it, is not material; it is enough that it contain'd in it the essence of all the love-romances which ever have been wrote since the beginning of the world. (8:22.575)

There are a number of suggestive parallels to the end of *Tristram Shandy* here: not only in the love affair and the oblique approaches, verbal and physical, to the genitals, but more specifically in the punning of the last line of Trim's story with its obvious sexual implications (like the cock and the bull), in the interruptiveness and inconclusiveness of the ending, and in Tristram's comment which, like Yorick's answer to Mrs. Shandy, lifts the referent (Toby's deflection) out of its immediate context, gives it broader and more literary implications, and bends a midair ending to a rounding off. Toby's remark is transformed into a comment on the entire "love-romance" that precedes and on all others like it, as Yorick's reply becomes a comment on the entire cock and bull story that precedes it, namely *Tristram Shandy*, "one of the best of its kind, I ever heard."

Likes create and engender their like. Sterne creates Tristram who tells of Trim who, with Toby's assistance, tells a tale remarkably like Tristram's own. The parallels between Trim's aborted tale of the king of Bohemia and Tristram's unwritable *Life and Opinions* are so many and so close that Sterne could not but have recognized and may very well have planned the replication. Just as the manner of its telling is a structural reproduction of the larger tale that includes it, the manner of its termination may very well have been intended as a calculated forewarning of the book's own puzzling and inconclusive closure. There is a strong likelihood, in other words, that at least as early as volume 8, published two years before the final volume, Sterne had a general sense, and perhaps more, of how his book must end.

## Analogues and Sources

In all this, *Tristram Shandy* presents us with a fictional correlative of the multilevel parallelism of music. With the possible exception of architecture, no art builds so conscientiously according to a design wherein the same patterns, principles, and materials echo and repeat themselves at successive levels of structure. "Musical form," writes Aaron Copland, ". . . resembles a series of wheels within wheels, in which the formation of the smallest wheel is remarkably similar to that of the largest one."[8]

Copland's observation is true in many and complex ways, but primarily in three major respects: procedurally, thematically, and intervallically. His main referent is procedural. Copland is speaking of the multileveled replication of the basic "repetitional principles" of music, exact repetition and repetition following a digression, that "apply both to the large sections which comprise an entire movement and also to the small units within each section."[9] The principle of exact repetition (a-a-a-a) that governs many songs, where long melodic lines are repeated precisely or nearly so, may also be operative within each line, determining the repetition of motives, phrases, and chords. And the massively inclusive ABA principle of exposition, development, and return which governs so-called "classical," "sonata," or "symphonic form" but which, as Heinrich Schenker has pointed out, is basic and permeative, hardly less natural to music than motion and sound,[10] will also be found at every lower order of structure as well, from the briefest sequence of passing tones in the exposition to the entire development section itself. The principle of repetition controls inner as well as outer form and does so on every plane.

Patterns of repetition, then, are themselves repeated at various levels of structure, but the principle of concentricity is no less substantive than procedural, as much a matter of the involuted repetition of chordal and thematic material as of patterns of repetition themselves. Themes may be rhythmically augmented or diminished, spatially contracted or expanded, or divided into simpler themes and motives of parallel construction, and some of these variants may appear within the scope and as part of the unfolding of larger ones. The same may be said of chordal material, the tones of a basic triad. Since the ABA sections of a sonata, for example, are traditionally governed by the tonic, dominant, and tonic keys respectively, ABA may also be written as I-V-I. Within each of these major sections will be numerous smaller segments elaborating the same progression, within these others of still narrower scope, and within these, chordal modifications of the basic triad or the triad itself. For Schenker the very essence of music lies in what he called *Auskomponierung* or "compositional unfolding" whereby the vertical chord, a harmonic concept, is horizontalized, gradually unfolded, and extended through time. The ultimate unity of the composition derives from the unfolding of a single chord, the determinant of tonality.[11] And "in this connection," writes one of Schenker's students, "it is fascinating to observe that such compositions in three parts, viewed as a whole, present a striking similarity to the construction of simple themes and sections, the single cells of the whole." Indeed the overall structure of the piece—its movement from I through V (or perhaps through II–V, III–V, or IV–V) and back to I—will be expressed in a single triad, in vertical space, and in a single moment in time.

The rough literary equivalents of procedural, thematic, and intervallic concentricity might be the onionskin repetitiveness of (respectively) narrative process, theme, and incident. *Tristram Shandy* is concentric in all three senses, though as in music they are overlapping, simultaneous, and often difficult to separate. The story of the king of Bohemia, for example, is an incident (though it is a horizontal progression rather than a single vertical moment[13]) imaging in confined space the total narrative effort, elaborating the themes of failed communication, frustrated narrative, solipsism, and the hobbyhorse, and illustrative of the pervasive procedure of statement, digression, and return. Much the same can be said of the explicitly musical segments of the novel—the seventh volume, the tuning of the orchestra, and the two sermons—and of a number of other incidents and sequences as well. For all that, *Tristram Shandy* is of course not as systematically concentric as a piece of music characteristically is. That would require a higher degree of repetitiveness than even a novel as musical as this one could possibly sustain and a higher order of rational structure than a mind like Tristram's could generate. But in this as in so many other ways, Sterne has stretched the limits of fiction toward the borderlines of music and overstepped them. *Tristram Shandy* is Ezekiel's vision as secular narrative.

The mind is an inherently repetitive instrument. Its methods and processes of perception, recollection, analysis, and formulation tend to take on characteristic and identifiable forms, to become habitual. "Nine parts in ten of a man's sense or his nonsense, his successes and miscarriages in this world depend upon [the] . . . motions and activity" of the animal spirits transfused at conception from father to child "and the different tracks and trains you put them into, so that when they are once set a-going . . . away they go cluttering like hey-go-mad; and by treading the same steps over and over again, they presently make a road of it" (1:1. 4–5). The same inevitably goes for a man's mental processes, his habits of association and communication (which help determine his "sense or nonsense"), so that what Tristram does once he is likely to do again; the patterns of thought, feeling, and narration that govern brief sequences are likely to govern longer ones, and what is true of the parts is likely to characterize the whole. If the mind thinks contrapuntally and in terms of simultaneous occurrence, it is as likely to do so in the handling of dialogue (or multilogue) as well as narration, scenically as well as panoramically, in the context of seconds or minutes as readily as days or months. If it works in terms of statement, departure, and return, beginning a story or philosophical thesis, fitfully reminding itself of unavoidable complications that dance or waft it away, and finally leaping or crawling its way back, the mind is as likely to follow that pattern within the bounds of a single incident or declamation as in the thematic development of the entire piece. And if Tristram is inclined to use repetition in the handling of theme, incident, or idea, we should not be surprised to find it at the level of word or phrase. All this is true of the mind of Tristram Shandy and, as a result, of the book he writes.

That is one explanation of the concentricity of *Tristram Shandy*, but it has another source, another purpose. Sterne may have put one sentence down and trusted to Almighty God for the next, but Almighty God is a masterful designer whose job it was, like Sterne's, to bring form out of chaos, not to perpetrate it. *Tristram Shandy* lives at the edge of chaos. But what has kept the book alive these two hundred years and more is, among other things, its well-hidden but well-constructed foundation—persistent processes and shapes, patterns of design and movement that hold it together and in place. Concentricity, the spiralling pattern of graduated replication and varied repetition, is another such formal pattern and like the others it can be fully explained only as a joint enterprise of formalism and realism. Shapes, events, ideas, and processes duplicate themselves in the mind and in the world, one experience echoes another, minor events are miniature variations of greater ones. But as with repetition, counterpoint, thematic variation, and the rest, the truth is heightened, stressed, given tighter shape, in short formalized for two main reasons: first to illuminate the patterns and special quality of experience, particularly interior experience, slighted by more conventional narrative; and second to provide this rebellious deviation from the norm with something to hang on to, with a form and structure—a largely musical form and structure—appropriate to its own eccentric needs. The formal in one sense may take precedence over the imitative: "be but in tune with yourself, madam, 'tis no matter how high or how low you take it." But since form is content in *Tristram Shandy*, since the processes of mind are both method and subject, the question of precedence may go unasked.

Tristram, as usual, is articulately aware of his achievement. His book, of course, antedates composer Aaron Copland's description of musical form by some two hundred years, but it is more than mere coincidence that Tristram describes the design of his book in exactly the same metaphor. Praising himself for the structural ingenuity of his composition, he writes, "I have constructed the main work and the adventitious parts of it with such intersections, and have so complicated and involved the digressive and progressive movements, one wheel within another, that the whole machine, in general, has been kept a-going" (1:22. 73). Tristram's claim is defensible on two grounds, both analogous to musical form and practice. One, the procedure he seems overtly concerned with in this remark, is the capacity to keep several parts simultaneously and interactively in motion either on separate lines or within a single continuously unfolding line, to sustain, depart, and progress at the same time, one often within the other. The second, implied by the metaphor and exhibited in his constant practice, is the subtle but striking procedural and substantive parallelism between the simultaneous and involuted parts. The first points to contrapuntalism, both to the spiralling concentricity of the work.

---

## The Musical Procedures

### Statement, development, and return

Perhaps the most striking example of procedural concentricity in *Tristram Shandy* and very likely the principal source of musical motion in Sterne's complex machine, is the confined application of the all-embracing pattern of statement, development, and return. In its broadest form this pattern helps structure the novel as a coherent unit, giving it a shape it seems determined to flee. It performs much the same function for many of the seemingly formless inner shapes, though at this lower order of structure the unity is often motivic rather than thematic, a matter of sentence, phrase, or minor idea rather than major subject or theme.

Take, for example, the following passage beginning with Tristram's account of Mrs. Wadman's strategies of pursuit:

Now as widow *Wadman* did love my uncle *Toby*——and my uncle *Toby* did not love widow *Wadman*, there was nothing for widow

Wadman to do, but to go on and love my uncle *Toby*——*or let it alone.*
  *Widow Wadman would do neither the one or the other.* (8:11. 549)

This last italicized portion (the italics, other than *Wadman* and *Toby*, are mine) states the central theme or main idea of the passage, and at this point the author digresses from its application to the Widow and develops it contrapuntally by relating it to himself:

Gracious heaven!——but I forget I am a little of her temper my-self; for whenever it so falls out, which it sometimes does about the equinoxes, that an earthly goddess is so much this, and that, and t'other, that I cannot eat my breakfast for her——and that she careth not three halfpence whether I eat my breakfast or no——
——Curse on her! (8:11.549-50)

With this, Tristram is off at a gallop contemplating the pernicious influence such goddesses, whom he cannot leave alone, have on his conduct. This in turn leads to a repudiation vibrant with sexual innuendo: "The duce take her and her influence too——for at that word I lose all patience ——much good may it do him!——By all that is hirsute and gashly! I cry, taking off my furr'd cap, and twisting it round my finger——I would not give sixpence for a dozen such!" (8:11.550). Here Tristram latches on to the implication of the double entendre (actually the implied meaning overwhelms the literal) and metaphorizes it: "But 'tis an excellent cap too (putting it upon my head, and pressing it close to my ears)——and warm——and soft; especially if you stroke it the right way——but alas! that will never be my luck——(so here my philosophy is shipwreck'd again)" (8:11.550).

We must keep in mind through all this that we are still on the development of the inability to take love or leave it

alone as this weakness applies to Tristram; and here, via
association, one obscene metaphor leads to another: "No,"
cries Tristram; "I shall never have a finger in the pye (so
here I break my metaphor)"; and dividing his new metaphorical idea into its component parts, as a composer might
fragment a melodic idea, he continues:

> Crust and Crumb
> Inside and out
> Top and bottom——I detest it, I hate it, I repudiate it——I'm
> sick at the sight of it——
>    'Tis all pepper,
>       garlick,
>       staragen,
>       salt, and
>       devil's dung——by the great arch cooks of cooks, who
> does nothing, I think, from morning to night, but sit down by the
> fire-side and invent inflammatory dishes for us, I would not touch
> it for the world. (8:11.550)

This last phrase has implications of its own, and like a composer strengthening and focusing attention on a musical
idea before developing it, Tristram repeats it: " 'Not touch
it for the world' did I say——" and then proceeds with the
new development:

> Lord, how I have heated my imagination with this metaphor!

> ### CHAP. XIII.
>
> Which shews, let your reverences and worships say what you will
> of it (for as for *thinking*——all who *do* think——think pretty
> much alike, both upon it and other matters)——LOVE is certainly,
> at least alphabetically speaking, one of the most
>   A gitating
>   B ewitching
>   C onfounded
>   D evilish affairs of life——the most

Extravagant
....(8:13.551)

Tristram takes love all the way through R, and by pushing the love theme, which he has really been playing with
all along, through virtually all the letters of the alphabet,
he achieves in effect a verbal correlative, or perhaps even
parody, of tonal modulation—through almost every possible key. The only reason Tristram doesn't make it all the
way to Z is that one of the implications of R changes his
direction. Appropriately enough, the word under R is Ridiculous, and it leads him to observe that "by the bye the
R should have gone first" (as perhaps it should have since
of all the "keys" this most accurately characterizes the love
theme as Tristram develops it here). Beginning with this
comment, Tristram effects a remarkable transition first into
a third polyphonic line (a conversation between the brothers Shandy) and then back to the tonic, his original point of
departure:

But in short 'tis of such a nature, as my father once told my uncle
*Toby* upon the close of a long dissertation upon the subject——
"You can scarce," said he, "combine two ideas together upon it,
brother *Toby*, without an hypallage"——What's that? cried my
uncle *Toby*.
   The cart before the horse, replied my father——
   ——And what has he to do there? cried my uncle *Toby*——
   Nothing, quoth my father, but to get in——*or let it alone.*
   Now widow *Wadman*, as I told you before, *would do neither
the one or the other.* (8:13.552; italics, except for names, mine)

In sum, the passage develops according to the following
pattern:
   1) STATEMENT: ". . . love my uncle Toby——or let it

alone. Widow Wadman would do neither the one or the other."

2) DEVELOPMENT in a different voice:

Application to Tristram
Repudiation or contrasting statement
Metaphorical association
Transition to second metaphorical association
Fragmentation of the metaphor into its component parts
Cadential or concluding statement of metaphor
Repetition of same
Development and modulation of implications of cadential phrase

3) RETURN:

Transition to a third voice, i.e., association of implications of last key with conversation between Walter and Toby
Repetition of opening statement.

This is no isolated instance. On the contrary, progression via the winding route of statement, development, and return, an almost inevitable by-product of Tristram's conflicting dedication to digressiveness on the one hand and to the autobiographical narrative on the other, is one of the distinctive marks and principal sources of the strange cyclical dynamic of the novel. Trim's persistent attempts to tell the story of the king of Bohemia, extending from volume 8, chapter 19 to volume 9, chapter 10, is likewise held together by the shoring pattern of statement, repeated departure, and stubborn return, as is the "prodigious armies" sequence beginning with 2:19 and ending in 3:6.

Following the line, "I wish, quoth my uncle *Toby*, you had seen what prodigious armies we had in Flanders," which ends the next to last chapter of volume 2, Tristram interrupts his story (we are at the time of his birth) to explain his father's mechanistic hypothesis about child delivery (it must be done feet-first to protect the vital and vulnerable "head-quarters of the soul" from the deliverer's forceps). The digression seems a radical departure, but in fact, like most of Tristram's digressions it is simultaneously progressive as well. Toby's "wish" is a hobbyhorsical interception of Dr. Slop's own, cutting off the doctor's parallel claim that "it would astonish you to know what Improvements we have made of late years in . . . the safe and expeditious extraction of the *foetus*." Toby interrupts the doctor to inform him of something related to his own obsession—warfare—only to be interrupted in turn by Tristram who would "remind [us] . . . of one thing"—his father's hobbyhorsical hypothesis about delivery—and "inform [us] . . . of another"—the structural ingenuity of his own vehicle, his book.[14] Only at the end of the digression (and the second volume) is it made clear that Walter's hypothesis is a direct explanation of the relevance of those forceps Slop was so proud of and of his insistence on hiring Slop as midwife (he too favors foot-first extraction), and that Toby's disorienting interjection was in fact symptomatic of that man's disapproval of this seeming perversion of nature and tradition.

Having thus wound his way back home, or rather having shown us how close by he'd really been all the time—he is like the child who runs away from home by running around the block—he can open his third volume, one year later, with a return to and repetition of the point of his narrative exodus. Actually it is not precisely the same point. Since stories do not always wait idly for the teller to get back to them, Tristram is obliged to make at least a minimal allowance for the time consumed by his digression; he has uncle Toby repeat the line presumably after a brief pause: " '*I wish*, Dr. *Slop*,' quoth my uncle *Toby* (repeating his wish for Dr. *Slop* a second time, and with a degree of more zeal and earnestness in his manner of wishing, than he had wished it at first)——'*I wish*, Dr. *Slop*,' quoth my uncle *Toby*, '*you had seen what prodigious armies we had in Flanders*' " (3:1.157). In this strange moving garden of live flowers where we must run at top speed merely to stay in the same place, the repetition assures us, first, that while we may not have "got some place" in the usual sense of that phrase, we have at least managed to hold our own, and second, that there is logic and a kind of order even on this side of the looking glass.

But this is still not the final recurrence of the line. The statement, generated as it is from nothing but the inner workings of Toby's mind, completely stymies Dr. Slop, and the dispute is halted for precisely four and one-half minutes by Tristram's calculation. "Five had been fatal to it," but Walter, fearful that the doctor's sputtering confusion will be the death of it,

took up the discourse as follows.

### CHAP. II.

"——What prodigious armies you had in *Flanders*!"——Brother *Toby*, replied my father. (3:1–2.158)

Here Tristram embarks on yet another series of digressions. All are as mechanistic and seemingly trivial as the argument they interrupt and, though they are in no other way recognizably relevant to the stated subject, all are in fact further variations on the mind-body theme. Again it is the restatement of the key phrase that ties it all together. Ultimately (four chapters later) Tristram winds his way back to an almost identical repetition of the principal lines:

my father at length went on as follows.

### CHAP. VI.

———"What prodigious armies you had in *Flanders!*"———Brother *Toby*, quoth my father. (3:5–6.163)

And Walter is off, mounting his hobbyhorse once more and riding away on his theme of delivery while Toby whistles "Lillabullero" into the next sequence. *Tristram Shandy*, externally referential for all its inward turning, is under more centripetal pressure than music is. But the mind of Tristram, rebellious thing that it is, strains against the pillars of conventional structure and threatens to reduce everything to confusion and debris. One of the internal forces inhibiting the urge to chaos is the recurrent pattern of statement, digression, and return, a small-scale model of cyclical development of the novel's major themes and the cyclical inclinations of its author's mind.

Within the pervasive AB(A) form, then, are smaller sections of parallel structure. Within these are others, smaller still. "The point to remember about these smaller units" of music, writes Aaron Copland, "is that every time a theme is exposed, there is strong likelihood that it will be repeated immediately; that once repeated, a digression is in order; and that after the digression, a return to the first theme, either exact or varied, is to be expected."[15] The following passage on real and psychological time follows so closely the pattern Copland outlines that it is worth quoting in full.

It is two hours, and ten minutes,——and no more,——cried my father, looking at his watch, since Dr. *Slop* and *Obadiah* arrived, ——and [statement:] I know not how it happens, brother *Toby*, ——but to my imagination it seems almost an age.

——Here——pray, Sir, take hold of my cap,——nay, take the bell along with it, and my pantoufles too.——

Now, Sir, they are all at your service; and I freely make you a present of 'em, on condition, you give me all your attention to this chapter.

Though my father said, [repetition:] "*he knew not how it happen'd,*"——yet [variant repetition:] he knew very well, how it happen'd;——and [digression:] at the instant he spoke it, was pre-determined in his mind, to give my uncle *Toby* a clear account of the matter by a metaphysical dissertation upon the subject of *duration and its simple modes*, in order to shew my uncle *Toby*, by what mechanism and mensurations in the brain it came to pass, that the rapid succession of their ideas, and the eternal scampering of discourse from one thing to another, since Dr. *Slop* had come into the room, had lengthened out so short a period, to so inconceivable an extent.——[return:] "I know not how it happens,—— cried my father,——but it seems an age." (3:18.188–89)

The procedure seems unmistakable, and it is but a compressed and salient instance of a pervasive mental and therefore narrative process. No less than the pattern of thematic development at the level of total integration, this more limited application tells us something about the mind. The mind does not work in a neat, orderly fashion, proceeding undisturbed from one idea to the next. On the contrary, beginning in one place it may find itself gradually drifting or suddenly transported elsewhere. It latches onto words, phrases, images, and concepts and (like a composer manipulating melodic fragments) varies and distorts them, proceeds either by association or some more mysterious force from one to the next, repeats them, varies their contexts, combines them with others that further increase the distance from its starting point, and through a combination of nature and effort, habitually though not invariably returns. The mind, particularly Tristram's, is a very multifarious organism indeed. No wonder he wishes that all who criticize him would pause first for a look inside his head.

## Repetition

The two basic principles of repetition in music are repetition after a digression and exact (or near immediate) repetition. In *Tristram Shandy*, as in the more complex musical forms, particularly the free forms, the former is dominant. But as part of that pattern and—to follow the winding spiral another turn toward the center—often within it on a lower order of structure, there is also an unusual degree of exact repetition as well.

No formal principle is more fundamental to music than repetition.

As long as musical sound consists solely of repetition, the monotone, it remains formless. On the other hand, when music goes to the other extreme and refuses to revert to any point, either rhythmic, melodic or harmonic, which recollection can identify, it is equally formless. Repetition and contrast, therefore, are the two twin principles of musical form. They are found asserting themselves in the most primitive examples of the folk tunes of all nations, and are not to be escaped from by the most daring innovators in modern music.[16]

Once a theme is stated it is likely to be repeated, and once the subsequent digression has been completed, the theme, in identical or varied form, will probably be repeated yet again. But repetition is almost as indispensable to the middle term, to development, as to statement and return. "Once a phrase has been stated, a great deal of its extension and development will take the form of repetition beginning on different degrees of the scale, in different registers, with different instruments, with alterations of time and intervals, with different harmonization—in fact, with any conceivable sort of variation, or often without any variation at all." [17] Repetition, as one musicologist puts it, is "a sort of natural state of music," [18] so basic, in fact, that many of the larger forms—fugue, rondo, and sonata, for example—cannot really be defined except in terms of repeated patterns. Exactly why repetition should play such a central role in almost all music is difficult to pin down, but one of the principal reasons also helps explain its role in *Tristram Shandy:* its reliance on internal relationships for meaning and order.

Music, like speech, is a human activity, but it is first of all a formalistic one, an art in which meaning and pleasure derive not, as in literature, from such largely "external" and conceptual criteria as credibility, truth to nature, psychological penetration into character and behavior, intellectual and philosophical profundity, depth and scope of moral vision, and so forth, but from the perception of internal relationships, from the occurrence, recurrence, and variation (tonal, contrapuntal, temporal, orchestral, harmonic, etc.) of moving patterns of sound. In such a context, repetition is not a violation of "how things happen" or "how people behave," but a deeply rooted formal convention of the art. And from this perspective, what was pleasant or satisfying once will in all probability be satisfying and pleasant again and yet again. Repetition provides, in other words, both the sense of formal interconnectedness and coherence we are listening for and, at the same time, a gratifying return to pleasing sound. Realistic fiction cannot sustain much repetition since precise or near precise repetition, if not comic or satiric, is simply not "realistic" in this sense, but a violation of that truth to nature—human and physical—we expect of such literature. Highly formalistic fiction, however— works like *The Waves* and *Between the Acts*, *Moderato Cantabile* and *The Square*, *Jealousy*, and *Last Year at Marienbad*, and of course *Tristram Shandy*—can sustain a good deal and offers, ideally, as much as it can profitably bear. The extensive use of repetition in these works is a step in their procession, if not necessarily a sign of their aspiration, toward the condition of music.

This is not to say that *Tristram Shandy* is or might be as repetitive as a fugue or rondo. True, Sterne's novel is more self-contemplative, more inward turning than traditional fiction; it places far greater stress on process than conventional prose; and it has wilfully abandoned many of the means the novel habitually uses to achieve the necessary sense of familiarity and order. But the medium of *Tristram Shandy* is, after all, language, its mode, in the end, mimetic, and the degree of repetition one finds, say, in Bach's violin Concerto no. 2 in E Major would be alien and ultimately destructive to it. Still, what describes the whole describes its parts. Just as Tristram can reassert at the end of his book the very subjects with which he began it, though in modified form, and just as a far greater degree of precise recapitulation—even total—would have made for an acceptable finale, he can make extraordinary use of repetition—exact or varied, immediate or delayed—on the level of sentence, phrase, or word. Each of the three passages cited above as evidence for Sterne's use of the pattern of statement, development, and return is an exhibit in this case as well. In the first, not only is the principal statement presented both at the beginning and end of the passage, but the paragraph which leads into and prepares us for the opening statement is itself uncommonly repetitive:

Now as widow Wadman DID LOVE *my uncle Toby*——and *my uncle Toby* DID NOT LOVE widow Wadman, there was nothing for widow Wadman to do, but to go on and LOVE *my uncle Toby* ——or let it alone.
Widow Wadman would do neither the one or the other.

In the untold tale of the king of Bohemia, repetition is equally pertinent and conspicuous. Over a span of only seven pages (8:19.560–66) the heading, "The Story of the king of Bohemia and his seven castles" and its sole variant "The story of the king of Bohemia and his seven castles, continued," appears no fewer than five times. Similarly, the first line of the story (and Trim gets only a very little way past it), "There was a certain king of *Bohemia*" or one of the several variations upon it, is repeated by the optimistic Trim four times in as many pages. In the last of the three sequences, the passages on duration and its simple modes, the statement, "I know not how it happens," along with two very slight modifications of it (one of them italicized) is reiterated three times in the space of twelve lines.

There are a great many more instances of concentrated repetition in *Tristram Shandy*. A particularly salient example is the "Fragment'" on the Lady Baussiere in which the line "The Lady Baussiere rode on" serves as a refrain repeated five times on a single page (5:1.346). Another is the comic tale of Margarita and the Abbess where the modest pair, faced with the problem of getting their recalcitrant mule moving without either having to utter the unspeakable curse that alone propels the beast, hit upon the evasion of dividing it between them. The episode is particularly interesting, not only for its extensive use of repetition, but for its remarkable rhythmic control and for the explicitly musical, more specifically antiphonic presentation:

Now I see no sin in saying, *bou, bou, bou, bou, bou,* a hundred times together; nor is there any turpitude in pronouncing the syllable *ger, ger, ger, ger, ger,* were it from our matins to our vespers: Therefore, my dear daughter, continued the abbess of *Andouillets* ——I will say *bou,* and thou shalt say *ger;* and then alternately, as there is no more sin in *fou* than in *bou*——Thou shalt say *fou*—— and I will come in (like fa, sol, la, re, mi, ut, at our complines) with *ter.* And accordingly the abbess, giving the pitch note, set off thus:

Abbess     ⎰ Bou- -bou- -bou- -
Margarita  ⎱ ——ger,- -ger,- -ger
Margarita  ⎰ Fou- -fou- -fou- -
Abbess     ⎱ ——ter,- -ter,- -ter.

The two mules acknowledged the notes by a mutual lash of their tails; but it went no further.——'Twill answer by an' by, said the novice.

Abbess     ⎰ Bou- bou- bou- bou- bou- bou-
Margarita  ⎱ ——ger, ger, ger, ger, ger, ger.

Quicker still, cried *Margarita.*

Fou, fou, fou, fou, fou, fou, fou, fou, fou.

Quicker still, cried *Margarita.*

Bou, bou, bou, bou, bou, bou, bou, bou, bou.

Quicker still——God preserve me! said the abbess——They do not understand us, cried *Margarita*——But the Devil does, said the abbess of *Andouillets.* (7:25.509–10)

And to cite but one further example of concentrated repetition, though there are many others,[19] there is the contrapuntal dialogue between uncle Toby and his man in which Trim, proposing the project on the bowling green for the first time, unfolds his vision in a linear progression over his master's excitedly repeated bass line. The passage is a classic verbal rendering of *basso ostinato:*

I would work under your Honour's directions like a horse, and make fortifications for you something like a tansy, with all their batteries, saps, ditches, and palisadoes, that it should be worth all the world's riding twenty miles to go and see it.

My uncle *Toby* blushed as red as scarlet as *Trim* went on;——but it was not a blush of guilt,——of modesty,——or of anger;——it was a blush of joy;——he was fired with Corporal *Trim's* project and description.——*Trim! said my uncle Toby, thou hast said enough.*——We might begin the campaign, continued *Trim,* on the very day that his Majesty and the Allies take the field, and demolish them town by town as fast as——*Trim, quoth my uncle Toby, say no more.*——Your Honour, continued *Trim,* might sit in your arm-chair (pointing to it) this fine weather, giving me your orders, and I would——*Say no more, Trim, quoth my uncle Toby.*——Besides, your Honour would get not only pleasure and good pastime,——but good air, and good exercise, and good health,——and your Honour's wound would be well in a month. *Thou hast said enough, Trim,*——*quoth my uncle Toby* (putting his hand into his breeches-pocket)——I like thy project mightily;——And if your Honour pleases, I'll, this moment, go and buy a pioneer's spade to take down with us, and I'll bespeak a shovel and a pick-ax, and a couple of——*Say no more, Trim, quoth my uncle Toby,* leaping up upon one leg, quite overcome with rapture,——and thrusting a guinea into *Trim's* hand,——*Trim, said my uncle Toby, say no more;*——but go down, *Trim,* this moment, my lad, and bring up my supper this instant. (2:5.97–98; except for names, my italics)

---

## Language, Rhetoric, and Emotion

Thus far the chapter's title metaphor has had a double application. The image of "wheels within wheels" refers both to the pervasive presence of musical principles and procedures at diminishing levels of composition and design and, more complexly, to the special relation beyond the shared general presence of music, of part to part and part to whole. As we narrow in on the more elementary components of the novel

—paragraph, sentence, phrase, and word—the relationship becomes less intricate but the musicality clearer and more explicit. The parts (with one exception) no longer comment quite so richly or directly on the overall structure or on other larger parts, but the remaining common element, the musicality itself, is more sharply defined and illuminated. Multiple reflection yields to double image and clearer definition, interpretation and speculation to simple pointing.

Sterne, as a practiced rhetorician, had a special interest in argumentation, and it is here that his keen sense of the rhetorical power of music (which he developed and refined in *A Sentimental Journey*) is most apparent. Subtleties of rhetorical implication and design are communicated everywhere through the metaphoric instrument of the music motif; the power of music to elicit, vary, or strategically define response is the assumption behind many of Tristram's musical allusions, metaphors, and techniques and behind Trim's persistent quest for his story's proper key. But music as rhetorical weapon is most frequently and most artfully employed in argument, where persuasion and the discriminate manipulation of response are paramount. Yorick wields it in his sermons—hence the strange musical notations that accompany them—and Walter is a virtuoso. He would take his hobbyhorsical subject of names over obstacles of indifference simply by laying his hand upon his antagonist's breast and addressing him in "that soft and irresistible *piano* of voice, which the nature of the *argumentum ad hominem* absolutely requires" (1:19.51). And should the discussion come round to the abhorrent name *Tristram*, his attack would become more aggressive though no less musical:

he would sometimes break off in a sudden and spirited EPI-PHONEMA, or rather EROTESIS, raised a third, and sometimes a

full fifth, above the key of the discourse,——and demand it cate-
gorically of his antagonist, Whether he would take upon him to
say, he had ever remember'd,——whether he had ever read,——
or even whether he had ever heard tell of a man, call'd *Tristram*,
performing any thing great or worth recording? (1:19.55)

In argument, as in almost everything else, uncle Toby
is the antithesis of his fractious brother. His arguments,
therefore, are almost never verbal. Instead, whenever anything strikes him as more than commonly absurd, Toby
expresses the ineffable by whistling a half dozen bars of
"Lillabullero." He whistles it, as we have seen, as a persistent accompaniment to Dr. Slop's reading of "Ernulphus's
Curse" over Obadiah. At one point in the reading,

[my uncle *Toby* taking the advantage of a *minim* in the second
barr of his tune, kept whistling one continual note to the end of
the sentence——Dr. *Slop* with his division of curses moving under
him, like a running bass all the way.] "May he be cursed in eating
and drinking, in being hungry, in being thirsty, in fasting, in
sleeping, in slumbering, in walking, in standing, in sitting, in lying, in working, in resting, in pissing, in shitting, and in blood-
letting."

"May he (*Obadiah*) be cursed in all the faculties of his body.

"May he be cursed inwardly and outwardly. . . .

"May he be damn'd in his mouth, in his breast, in his heart and
purtenance, down to the very stomach.

"May he be cursed in his reins, and in his groins," (God in
heaven forbid, quoth my uncle *Toby*)——"in his thighs, in his
genitals," (my father shook his head) "and in his hips, and in his
knees, his legs, and feet, and toenails. . . .

"May the Son of the living God, with all the glory of his Majesty"——[Here my uncle *Toby* throwing back his head, gave a
monstrous, loud, loud Whew——w——w——something betwixt
the interjectional whistle of *Hey day!* and the word itself. . . .]
(3:11.175–77; brackets in the text)

Wheels within wheels, Dr. Slop's running bass echoing the
one that permeates the novel generally, uncle Toby's whis-

tled commentary echoing Tristram's verbal intrusions over the running bass of his story. Both in a sense are musical attempts to express the ineffable. Tristram's intrusions—his digressive anecdotes, hypotheses, and frustrations—are a kind of extended "Lillabullero," a running commentary on the inexpressible absurdity of our condition.

One of the mildest of men, uncle Toby habitually avoids direct confrontations with his contentious brother. A few bars of "Lillabullero" is usually enough to release his frustration, make his point, and keep the peace. But other, more antagonistic responses are possible if not forthcoming. Walter's harsh repetition of Toby's "what prodigious armies" interjection is an invitation to an orchestrated clash of instruments, but Toby declines it. Any other man, as Tristram points out,

observing the prodigious suffusion of blood in my father's countenance, ... the violent knitting of my father's brows, and the extravagant contortion of his body during the whole affair,——would have concluded my father in a rage; and taking that for granted, ——had he been a lover of such kind of concord as arises from two such instruments being put into exact tune,——he would instantly have skrew'd up his, to the same pitch;——and then the devil and all had broke loose——the whole piece, madam, must have been played off like the sixth of Avison Scarlatti——*con furia,*——like mad.——Grant me patience!——What has *con furia,*——*con strepito,*—— or any other hurlyburly word whatever to do with harmony? (3:5.163)

The "instrument" referred to here is the human body, principally the physiognomy. The knitting of brows, the rising of color, and various contortions of the face and body are all forms of rhetorical communication which, like uncle Toby's *Argumentum Fistulatorium,* substitute for and often transcend ordinary language.[20] The most common and affective instrument, however, is the human voice. By means of a large number of metaphorical descriptions of human speech—Walter's *piano* of voice is but one of many instances—Tristram establishes an unmistakable correspondence between the human voice and a musical instrument, between verbal language and the language of music. Music, in other words, is present in *the* basic component of *Tristram Shandy* (or any other literary work)—language. Even the single word (and note the word that stimulates Tristram's speculation) may be musically expressive: "Now there are such an infinitude of notes, tunes, cants, chants, airs, looks, and accents [Tristram reflects] with which the word *fiddlestick* may be pronounced in all such causes as this, every one of 'em impressing a sense and meaning as different from the other, as *dirt from cleanliness*" (9:25. 635). The musicality of the single word, and indeed of discourse in general, is evident in Phutatorius's painful encounter with the boiling chestnut.

ZOUNDS!———————————————————

————Z——ds! cried *Phutatorius*, partly to himself——and yet high enough to be heard——and what seemed odd, 'twas uttered in a construction of look, and in a tone of voice, somewhat between that of a man in amazement, and of one in bodily pain.

One or two who had very nice ears, and could distinguish the expression and mixture of the two tones as plainly as a *third* or a *fifth*, or any other chord in musick——were the most puzzled and perplexed with it——the *concord* was good in itself——but then 'twas quite out of the key, and no way applicable to the subject started;——so that with all their knowledge, they could not tell what in the world to make of it.

Others who knew nothing of musical expression, and merely lent their ears to the plain import of the *word*, imagined that *Phutatorius*, who was somewhat of a cholerick spirit, was just going to snatch the cudgels out of *Didius's* hands, in order to bemawl *Yorick* to some purpose. (4:27.318)

But these metaphors, like almost all the musical metaphors of the book, are signs as well as instruments. Their
implications overflow their space like an arrow or a pointing
finger, and what they point to is one of the few elements
of Sterne's musicality that has been widely observed and
amply treated: the rich distinctive musicality of his prose,
of his own language as much as—more than—Walter's,
Elizabeth's, Toby's, Trim's, Phutatorius's, or any of the rest.
In his *Dialogues de l'Eloquence*, Fénelon wrote that "due
pronunciation is a kind of music; whose beauty consists in
the variety of proper tones and inflexions of the voice, which
ought to rise or fall with a just and easy cadence, according
to the nature of things we express."[21] The tones and inflexions, the rise and fall of the voice are one part of the
musicality of speech and of Sterne's conversational style,
and they are suggested not only by music metaphors (*piano,
fortissime, grave,* a third or a fifth above the key of the discourse, and so forth), but by the pervasive and characteristic
use of the exclamation point, dashes of varying lengths,
italics, parentheses, spacing, capitals, various type sizes and
typefaces, and so on. More important however, is the movement, the break of flow, the shifting contours of the prose
which is everywhere a reflection of mood and impulse,
feeling and thought. The movement can be felt, for example, in the rhythm, in the constantly changing intensity
and length of the more than three hundred chapters of the
book. The chapters, like all else, follow the flow of thought
and feeling, sometimes sprawling out over ten, fifteen, or
twenty pages and covering almost as many years, sometimes
tumbling over one another, two or three to a page, and
offering hardly more than a sentence or two and a brief,
fleeting moment in time:

Brother *Shandy*, answered my uncle *Toby*, looking wistfully in his face,——you are much mistaken in this point;——for you do increase my pleasure very much, in begetting children for the *Shandy* family at your time of life.——But, by that, Sir, quoth Dr. *Slop*, Mr. *Shandy* increases his own.——Not a jot, quoth my father.

### CHAP. XIII.

My brother does it, quoth my uncle *Toby*, out of *principle*.——In a family-way, I suppose, quoth Dr. *Slop*.——Pshaw!——said my father,——'tis not worth talking of.

### CHAP. XIV.

. . .

(2:12–14.115–16)

And the rhythms within the chapters are as variable as the rhythms that join them, their tones and styles as varied as either. They range from the academic and pedantic to the discursive and colloquial, from baroque statelines to *galant* volatility, from sobriety and pathos to gaiety and absurdity, and from frenzy to serenity. The chapters, as Henri Fluchére observes, "are divided up solely in accordance with an interior rhythm which the commentary accompanying the 'story' imposes upon it. Each has, or almost, its own unity of content, as of tone and rhythm."[22]

In the microcosmic mirror-world of *Tristram Shandy*, descriptions are ubiquitous, and what holds for the chapters holds everywhere for the prose in general. The characteristic Shandean sentence is not primarily a grammatical unit of designative meaning, but an emotive complex of internal motion and tension. It is not so much a logical ordering of linguistic signs as a moving pattern of thought and impulse, a complex arrangement of rhythmic units creating, complicating, and resolving tensions (or refusing to), and communicating a great deal more than it ever says.

*Pray, my dear,* quoth my mother, *have you not forgot to wind up the clock?*——*Good G——!* cried my father, making an exclamation, but taking care to moderate his voice at the same time,——*Did ever woman, since the creation of the world, interrupt a man with such a silly question?* Pray, what was your father saying?—— Nothing. (1:1.5)

The HOMUNCULUS, Sir, in how-ever low and ludicrous a light he may appear, in this age of levity, to the eye of folly or prejudice: ——to the eye of reason in scientifick research, he stands confess'd ——a BEING guarded and circumscribed with rights:——The minutest philosophers, who, by the bye, have the most enlarged understandings, (their souls being inversely as their enquiries) shew us incontestably, That the HOMUNCULUS is created by the same hand,——engender'd in the same course of nature,——endowed with the same loco-motive powers and faculties with us:——That he consists, as we do, of skin, hair, fat, flesh, veins, arteries, ligaments, nerves, cartilages, bones, marrow, brains, glands, genitals, humours, and articulations;——is a Being of as much activity, ——and, in all senses of the word, as much and as truly our fellow-creature as my Lord Chancellor of England. (1:2.5)

But in this clear climate of fantasy and perspiration, where every idea, sensible and insensible, gets vent——in this land, my dear *Eugenius*——in this fertile land of chivalry and romance, where I now sit, unskrewing my ink-horn to write my uncle *Toby's* amours, and with all the meanders of JULIA'S track in quest of her DIEGO, in full view of my study window——if thou comest not and takest me by the hand——

What a work is it likely to turn out! Let us begin it. (8:1.539)

Phrases, sentences, and paragraphs rise and fall like musical phrases, figures, and subjects; they pulsate, accent, fade to silence, accelerate and slacken off, increase and diminish in length and volume, gather tension and release it, flow and stop and flow again. In all this, punctuation—particularly the dash—is perhaps Sterne's most effective and most conspicuously musical, though by no means his only tool.

(Note too his use of upper case, italics, and the list.) Sterne "punctuates heavily," observes Samuel Monk, "so as to indicate, as would a composer, the rests and pauses that are essential to attaining expressive rhythms."[23] His dashes are not, as dashes are wont to be, all of a length. Rather, as Sterne uses them, they are like musical rests, barlines, or *sostenuti*, lengthening, measuring off, marking pauses, emphases, and directional shifts, varying in length to suit his changing needs and capturing graphically the multiple rhythms of mind, activity, and speech and the strange suggestiveness of silence.[24] Like their musical counterparts, then, Sterne's linguistic units are in constant flux and pulsing motion, changing size and shape, intensity, velocity and tone, flowing into, through, and out of one another—all "to snatch a grace from music" and so express—through language as well as subject, through signs as well as what they signify—the subtle nuances of shifting moods, sensations, thoughts, and feelings:

CRACK, crack——crack, crack——crack, crack——so this is *Paris!* quoth I (continuing in the same mood)——and this is *Paris!*—— humph!——*Paris!* cried I, repeating the name the third time——
     The first, the finest, the most brilliant——
     ——The streets however are nasty;
     But it looks, I suppose, better than it smells——crack, crack—— crack, crack——What a fuss thou makest!——as if it concern'd the good people to be inform'd, That a man with a pale face, and clad in black, had the honour to be driven into *Paris* at nine o'clock at night, by a postilion in a tawny yellow jerkin turned up with red calamanco——crack, crack——crack, crack——crack, crack——I wish thy whip——
     ——But 'tis the spirit of thy nation; so crack——crack on.
     Ha!——and no one gives the wall!——but in the SCHOOL of URBANITY herself, if the walls are besh-t——how can you do otherwise?
     And prithee when do they light the lamps? What?——never

in the summer months!——Ho! 'tis the time of sallads.——O rare! sallad and soup——soup and sallad——sallad and soup, *encore* ——'Tis too much for sinners. (7:17.498–99)

Sterne's prose, both by metaphorical implication and, far more importantly, by the evidence of its own presentation, is emphatically musical, and the analogy deepens as it grows. According to eighteenth-century physiological psychology, human utterances were audible signs of the vibrations of the nerves, the internal receptors and transmitters of human emotion. "Certain vocal tones," wrote James Beattie, "accompany certain mental emotions."[25] And Sterne enriches his voice-instrument metaphor with a further identification (it is more than a mere analogue or parallel) between the source of vocal tone—the human emotions—and a musical instrument. Predictably, this supportive identification appears most often in the more sentimental passages of the novel, the encounter with Maria, for example, when "I was in the most perfect state of bounty and good will; and felt the kindliest harmony vibrating within me" (9:24.629);[26] and uncle Toby's benevolent liberation of the fly:

I was but ten years old when this happened; but whether it was, that the action itself was more in unison to my nerves at that age of pity, which instantly set my whole frame into one vibration of most pleasurable sensation;——or how far the manner and expression of it might go towards it;——or in what degree, or by what secret magic,——a tone of voice and harmony of movement, attuned by mercy, might find a passage to my heart, I know not;——this I know, that the lesson of universal good-will then taught and imprinted by my uncle *Toby*, has never since been worn out of my mind. (2:12. 113–14)

What these metaphors collectively suggest is a quite literal view of the human animal as an instrument of musical expression and response. The voice is a musical instrument because the vocal chords vibrate sympathetically with the super-sensitive nerve fibers whose vibrations are the indices and determinants of emotion. The body (or human frame) which houses these vibrating strings is itself an instrument capable of reflecting the interior motions not only in sound but in silent though hardly less expressive changes of physiology and physiognomy—the knitting of the brows, the flush of the countenance, the contortions of the body, and the thousand pregnant gestures with which all the characters of the novel—Trim most habitually and effectively —express themselves.

Clearly, the rhetorical function of music in *Tristram Shandy* is fully compatible with the procedural and structural. The music motif, insisting on correspondences between music and musical instruments on the one hand, voice, body, and feeling on the other, reinforces the musical motion and structure of *Tristram Shandy* by insisting on the musicality of the very stuff of which this or any other novel is made; it turns the novel's characters into expressive instruments, their language into musical tones and rhythms capable of both expressing and eliciting a wide variety of feelings, emotions, and moods. The conceptual and nondesignative meanings and implications of fluid motion, contrapuntalism, thematic development, repetition, and concentricity are inevitably complemented, deepened, and intensified by the musicality of character, feeling, and expression. In fact it is this pervasive and complementary presence of musical vocabulary and metaphors—made possible by the fertile if antiquated vibration theory of emotion —that in large part accounts for the richer and more sensible musicality of *Tristram Shandy* as contrasted with more modern musical novels like *Steppenwolf, Point Counter Point*, and *The Counterfeiters*. The ordering of prose, even extraordinary prose, into contrapuntal patterns, fugal or sonata form, or the like is ultimately a less richly musical enterprise than the comparable ordering of a prose that, through a combination of sound and reflexive suggestion (metaphoric self-description) strives at the same time for the illusion of musical tones emanating from musical instruments. There is little sense in *Tristram Shandy* of analogy largely for the abstract sake of analogy or the dry sake of achievement and proof. The materials as well as the form and manner of the book are musical, and the result, when Sterne and his readers are working sympathetically, is a rich intermixture of musical meaning and effect.

The rhetorical use of music's emotive power suggests a final explanation for the presence of music in Sterne's novel. To a very considerable degree, *Tristram Shandy* is a book about the problem of communication. The novel rises, expands and mis-takes shape out of the author's own largely frustrated attempts to communicate his feelings, opinions, and autobiography to his readers, and concerns itself with the similarly frustrated attempts of its characters to establish meaningful communication among themselves. Because it is a book concerned largely with communication (or the lack of it), and because one of the primary communicative acts in the novel is the narrator's own half-realized attempts to make personal contact with his readers, the narrative style is extraordinarily conversational and familiar. "Writing," Tristram insists, ". . . is but a different name for conversation," and style reflects belief. Tristram personally and intimately addresses the reader as "Sir" or "Madam," "your worship" or "your reverence"; gently collars him in order to let him in on one or another of his private observations about art or nature; invites him into his den to watch him wrestle with the monstrous problems of autobiography; and even urges the reader to join the battle by filling in missing words or supplying a picture of the delectable Widow Wadman on a blank page provided for the purpose. In an important sense, the book is a friendly if troubled conversation between Tristram and his readers, the end result of which is an almost unprecedented intimacy between author and reader.

This is precisely Sterne's intent. To him and to Tristram genuine communication extends beyond the mere transference of words across space. Its purpose is not so much to convince the mind as to strike upon the heart and let the brain run after it, to involve, engage, cajole, affect, and so create between author and reader a communication that reaches through the vagueness, imprecision, and inadequacy of mere words to the roots of feeling and response. The "unsteady use of words," Tristram tells us, "have perplexed the clearest and most exalted understandings" (2:2.86), for words, he has learned from Locke, "*stand for nothing but the ideas in the mind of him that uses them.*"[27] They do not represent objective reality, but are merely "the signs of men's ideas," and as such they may imperfectly suggest the ideas they are intended to represent and may be open to a variety of interpretations. Sterne is at war with mere words because they cannot do his work. Tristram's persistent and overriding aim therefore is not verbal precision and complete conceptual understanding; these are impossible and, even if achieved, less than enough. Rather he seeks the emotional rapport, the empathic contact and identification that will "convey but the same impressions to every other brain, which the occurrences themselves excite in my own" (4:27.337). This is the kind of communication Tristram hopes for, and it is the only kind he or his characters ever really achieve. Walter and Toby manage almost no intellectual contact whatever—far less in fact than Tristram and his readers enjoy. But more important, like Tristram and his audience, they do achieve a deepening empathy, an affectionate if inarticulable comprehension of the workings of each other's mind and heart. The book's main object, writes Fluchère,

> is to persuade the reader of the reality of an intellectual activity in progress, or an emotional state in process of dissolution, or the imaginary representation of an action and characters drawn from the past but reinstated in the present—to convince him of all this and to ensure his co-operation in the verbal re-creation of a figurative universe. This imagery was to be more than the symbol of the intellectual activity, it was to be the activity itself in its full development.[28]

Tristram's aim is not to tell, but to urge, not to sell ideas— even clearly defined ideas—but to share an activity and an experience; and his ends cannot be gained with words alone. They are gained only with the indispensable aid of physical attitude, gesture, facial expression, poignant silence, and the sound, the music, the rhythms, and tones of the human voice. If writing is conversation and if, as is clearly the case, conversation properly managed is at least as much a musical and dramatic art as a verbal or linguistic one, then it becomes the business of the book—the very troublesome but uncannily successful business of the book—to squeeze music and gesture into print, to elicit from the limited resources of ink and page the rhetorical efficacy of drama and music. Walter Shandy, the master of rhetorical disputation, understands full well the strange affective potency of the musical;

hence the *piano* of voice that the *argumentum ad hominem* requires, the *erotesis* raised a third or full fifth above the key of discourse. Trim, the master of the rhetorical gesture and the sentimental narrative, senses it instinctively; hence the modulation of his tale into the key that gives it sense and spirit and that suits his auditor's mood. And Tristram, the rhetorical master of masters, grasps it totally; hence, in part at least, the musical prose, form, and matter of his book.

One can explain the presence of musical forms, techniques, and language in *Tristram Shandy* in a number of ways: as a means of presenting the image of life as ongoing process, the patterns and complexities of consciousness, simultaneity within and between the interior and external worlds; as a means of conveying the immediacy, continued presentness, and fluid evanescence of time; as a vehicle for expressive communication, empathic identification, and sentimental effects. But whatever may have brought music to *Tristram Shandy*, it performs, in varying degrees, all these services and it permeates the novel.

Music is present, in fact, at every level of construction from the most abstract and inclusive procedural principles to the smallest concrete component, in every wheel, digressive and progressive, that turns within and around other wheels to keep the book in motion. Beginning, to start with the innermost element, with the germinal analogy indentifying the human frame with the stringed instrument, it works its way outward through a like correlation between the human voice and a musical instrument and, as a result, between human language and the language of music, including keys, pitch, notes, rests, stresses, and dynamics. It makes itself felt in both the implied and flourished correlation of conversations, arguments, and narrative passages with comparable musical sequences, of chapters with musical interludes and volumes with movements. Music is also and perhaps most significantly present in such formal procedures as repetition and contrast; transition, modulation and variation; statement, development, and recapitulation, concentricity and counterpoint. And finally, music is implicit in the improvisatory virtuosity of *Tristram Shandy*, in its fluid shape and motion, and in its uniquely thorough and complex coalescence of subject and process, content and form.

Robert Bridges, discussing the possibility of an effective marriage of music and poetry, listed a number of obstacles to their satisfactory union: music's demand for more repetition than poetry (and certainly prose) can tolerate; the tendency of a musical composition to conclude with a recapitulation of its opening passages; the difficulty of adjusting the rhythms of music to the rhythms of language; and the difficulty of reconciling the definite and controlled denotations and connotations of literature with the indefinite but stronger emotional suggestiveness of music.[29] Bridges's immediate concern was the problem of providing an appropriate musical setting for a poem, but his remarks are equally pertinent if less exhaustive as applied to any effort to "musicalize" prose fiction. The relevant point is that in *Tristram Shandy* Sterne narrowed each of these major gaps between the sister arts and a number of others besides.

Every reader of *Tristram Shandy* leaves it with the feeling that he has had a most uncommon experience with a most uncommonly written, oddly constructed work of fiction. The feeling is as justified as it is unsettling, and together with much of the "musicalized" poetry and fiction of the past century and a half, it is traceable to the pervasive musicality of Sterne's precocious novel. In the end, these pages notwithstanding, *Tristram Shandy* remains in unusual and important measure ineffable. But then again, that was pretty much their point.

# Notes

## Chapter 1
## Introduction: Music and Fiction

1. Calvin Brown, *Music and Literature: A Comparison of the Arts* (Athens: University of Georgia Press, 1948), pp. 213–17. See also H. A. Basilius, "Thomas Mann's Use of Musical Structure and Techniques in Tonio Kröger," *Germanic Review* 19 (December 1944): 284–308.

2. Thomas Mann, Preface to *Stories of Three Decades*, trans. H. T. Lowe-Porter (New York: Alfred A. Knopf, 1936), p. vi.

3. Paul Emile Cadilhac, Preface to *La Pastorale*, cited in Brown, *Music and Literature*, p. 174.

4. Hermann Hesse, *Der Kurgast, Betrachtungen, Gesammelte Dichtungen* (Berlin-Zurich: Suhrkamp Verlag, 1957) 4: 113; Theodore Ziolkowski, "Hermann Hesse's Steppenwolf: A Sonata in Prose," *Modern Language Quarterly* 19 (1958): 115–40.

5. See Ramon Fernandez, *André Gide* (Paris: Correa, 1931), pp. 152–54 for a discussion of the musical pattern of thematic repetition and development in *Les Faux-Monnayeurs*.

6. See L.A.G. Strong, *The Sacred River: An Approach to James Joyce* (London, Methuen, 1949), pp. 44–51 for a discussion of the sirens section as fugue; see particularly the Anna Livia Plurabelle section of *Finnegans Wake* and Melvin Friedman's discussion of it on p. 241 of his *Stream of Consciousness: A Study in Literary Method* (New Haven: Yale University Press, 1955).

7. Respectively, Ezra Pound, in *Polite Essays* (London: Faber and Faber, 1937), and Joseph Warren Beach, *Twentieth Century Novel: Studies in Technique* (New York: Appleton-Century, 1932), p. 418.

8. André Gide. *The Counterfeiters*, trans. Dorothy Bussy (Harmondsworth, Middlesex: Penguin Books, 1966 [originally published as *Les Faux-Monnayeurs*, France, 1925]), p. 171. Gide

provides a clearer sense of what he may have had in mind and why in the December 7, 1921 entry to his *Journals:*

> Every evening I plunge again, for a half-hour, into the *Kunst der Fugue.* Nothing I said of it the other day strikes me as quite exact now. No, one does not often feel in it either serenity or beauty, but rather an intellectual torment and an effort of the will to bend forms as rigid as laws and inhumanly inflexible. It is the triumph of the mind over figures; and, before the triumph, the struggle. And while submitting to restraint—through it, in spite of it, or *thanks to it*—all the play of emotion, of tenderness, and, after all, of harmony that can still remain (*The Journals of André Gide*, 2 vols., trans. and ed. Justin O'Brien [New York: Vintage Books, 1956], 1:311).

9. Wilhelm Heinrich Wackenroder and Ludwig Tieck, *Phantasien über die Kunst, für Freunde der Kunst* (1799). Cited in *Kunstanschauung der Frühromantik*, ed. Andreas Muller (Leipzig: Philipp Reclam, 1931), p. 114.

10. Helen Moglen, "Laurence Sterne and the Contemporary Vision," in *The Winged Skull: Essays on Laurence Sterne*, Arthur H. Cash & John M. Stedmond, eds. (London: Methuen, 1971), p. 70.

11. Wellek and Warren, *Theory of Literature* (New York: Harcourt, Brace, 1949 [first printing 1942]), p. 231.

12. Robert Gorham Davis, "Sterne and the Delineation of the Modern Novel," in *The Winged Skull*, p. 23.

13. Edmund Burke, *Philosophical Inquiry into the Origin of Our Ideas of the Sublime and Beautiful*, ed. James T. Boulton and Kegan Paul (London: Routledge, 1958 [originally published 1757]), p. 120.

14. See K. E. Gilbert and Helmut Kuhn, *A History of Esthetics* (Bloomington: University of Indiana Press, 1953), 205–15; Arthur Locke, "Descartes and 17th Century Music," *Musical Quarterly* 21 (1935): 423–31; and John Hollander, *The Untuning of the Sky* (New York: W. W. Norton, 1970), especially chapters 4 and 6.

15. Anthony Ashley Cooper, third earl of Shaftesbury, *Characteristics of Men, Manners, Opinions, Times, etc.*, 2 vols., ed. James Robertson (Gloucester, Mass.: P. Smith, 1963 [Reprint of 1900 edition; originally published 1732]), 1:154.

16. Quoted in Stanley Burnshaw, *The Seamless Web* (New York: George Braziller, 1970), p. 140.

17. Immanuel Kant, *Critique of Judgment*, trans. J. H. Bernard

(London: Macmillan, 1914 [originally published 1790]), p. 217.

18. Ernest Newman, *Gluck and the Opera* (London: V. Gollancz, 1964 [originally published 1895]), pp. 285–86.

19. See Walter Jackson Bate, *From Classic to Romantic*, (New York: Harper Brothers, 1961), pp. 149–50.

20. For the influence of painting on *Tristram Shandy* and *A Sentimental Journey*, see particularly Wilbur Cross, *The Life and Times of Laurence Sterne*, 3rd ed. (New Haven: Yale University Press, 1929), p. 114; Walter Watkins, *The Perilous Balance* (Princeton: Princeton University Press, 1939), pp. 146–52; and William Holtz, "Typography, *Tristram Shandy*, The Aposiopesis, etc." in *The Winged Skull*, pp. 248–50. "That Sterne was a painter before he wrote *Tristram Shandy*," Cross observes, "must have been surmised by every reader of the book; for he therein employs so easily the technical terms of the art for running up parallels on the mechanics of literary expression, or for describing the poise and movement of his characters."

For the influence of drama and the dramatic character of *Tristram Shandy*, see for example Watkins, p. 147; Holtz pp. 251–55; and John Traugott, *Tristram Shandy's World: Sterne's Philosophical Rhetoric* (Berkeley and Los Angeles: University of California Press, 1954), p. 130. "*Tristram Shandy*," writes Holtz, "is essentially dramatic: it consists almost entirely of monologue and dialogue; Tristram alternately presents scenes from his family history and steps before the curtains to engage his readers in a one-sided colloquy. . . . Always between us and the fictive world stands Sterne the showman, a painter before he took up the pen, who conducts his writing like a dramatic performance wherein he can paste up drawings and emblems as accessories to his narrative."

21. In purely numerical terms, music would seem to have the strongest support. See, for example, Walter Sichel, *Sterne: A Study* (Philadelphia: J. B. Lippincott, 1910), p. 176; Margaret Shaw, *Laurence Sterne: The Making of a Humorist, 1713–1762* (London: Richard Press, 1957), p. 189; Samuel Monk, Introduction to *The Life and Opinions of Tristram Shandy, Gentleman* (New York: Rinehart, 1950), p. xix; A. A. Mendilow, *Time and the Novel* (New York: Humanthes Press, 1952), pp. 180–81; Alan Dugald McKillop, *The Early Masters of English Fiction* (Lawrence, Kansas: University of Kansas Press, 1956); and Jean-Jacques Mayoux, "Variations on the Time-sense in *Tristram Shandy*," in *The Winged Skull*, p. 13. These and others have made mention of Sterne's con-

trapuntal or "polyphonic technique" (Mendilow, McKillop, and Monk), "variations on recurrent themes" and musical "rests and pauses" (Monk), the "musical linking of his phrases and delicate variations of tone and tempo" (Shaw), and his insistence on the general "musical character, rhythm and tempos of literary creation" (Mayoux). But none of these insights have been developed beyond a sentence or two; a disproportionate stress has been placed on musical sound rather than pattern and technique; and not everyone agrees that music is a significant factor in the novel at all.

At least one commentator has explicitly and quite surprisingly rejected the notion of a musical presence or influence in *Tristram Shandy*. Following a perceptive analysis of stream-of-consciousness fiction, of the importance of music to the form, and of the unique and multiple contributions of *Tristram Shandy* to its development, Melvin Friedman (*Stream of Consciousness*, pp. 29–30) declares that the analogy with Sterne's novel is "certainly with the visual art of painting. . . . Despite Sterne's training in music," he goes on, "there are probably no formal borrowings from this art." The logic is tenable. Both music and *Tristram Shandy* may be crucial factors in the development of the stream-of-consciousness novel without their having anything more in common. But in the light of Friedman's own description of stream-of-consciousness fiction, *Tristram Shandy*, the possible literary uses of music, and the obvious link through Bergson, the conclusion is, as I say, surprising. It is also, as I hope to show, untrue.

22. Ralph Freedman, *The Lyrical Novel: Studies in Hermann Hesse, André Gide, and Virginia Woolf* (Princeton, New Jersey: Princeton University Press, 1966), see especially chapter 1.

23. Ibid., p. 273.

24. John Cowper Powys, Introduction to *Tristram Shandy* (London: Macdonald Illustrated Classics, 1949), p. 7.

25. Sterne subscribed to the concerts in the Assembly rooms at York in 1764 and was a member of the "Society," an exclusive group of subscribers for whom Theresa Cornelys arranged her famous assemblies at Carlisle House from 1760–1772. His letters often refer to and describe concerts he planned to attend or had attended. See, for example, Sterne to Catherine Fourmantel, 8 [March] 176[0], in *Letters of Laurence Sterne*, ed. Lewis Perry Curtis (Oxford: Clarendon Press, 1935), p. 97; Sterne to Lord Fauconberg, 16 January 1767, ibid., p. 296; Sterne to Mr. and Mrs.

William James, ? [3 January 1768], ibid., p. 409; and Sterne to Mr. and Mrs. James ? [4 January 1768], ibid.

In London he made the acquaintance of the musical Duke of York, supped with him, and accompanied him to concerts where the duke performed on the violin. In Naples he spent much of his time with Mr. and Mrs. Hamilton, of whom Walpole wrote, "[She is] as musical as he is connoisseur" (*Letters*, p. 274).

In a letter probably written in June, 1761, Sterne wrote Mrs. Vesey:

> That you are graceful, & elegant & most desirable &c &c. every common beholder, who only stares at You as a dutch Boore does at the Queen of Sheba in a puppit Show can readily find out; But that You are sensible, and gentle and tender—& from one end to the other of you full of the sweetest tones & modulations, requires a Connoisseur of more taste & feeling—in honest truth You are a System of harmonic Vibrations—You are the sweetest and best tuned of all Instruments. . . . the deuce take you w$^h$ your musical and other powers—could nothing serve you but you must turn T. Shandys head, as if it was not turn'd enough already: as for turning my heart; I forgive You, as you have been so good as to turn it towards so excellent & heavenly an Object. (Ibid., p. 138)

26. See, for example, Sterne to the Reverend Robert Browne, 9 September 1760, ibid., p. 122; Sterne to Robert Foley, 17 December 1762, ibid., p. 191; and the passage in his "Memoirs of the Life and Family of the Late Rev. Mr. Laurence Sterne" (1767), ibid., p. 4. An anecdotist cited by Sterne's biographer, Wilbur Cross, speaks of gatherings at the rectory and neighboring houses at Sutton where Sterne played the bass viol for friends, and Sterne's friend, John Hall Stevenson, president of the "Demoniacs" of "Crazy Castle" where Sterne spent much of his time, writes that Laurence habitually "fell to fiddling" (Cross, *Life and Times*, pp. 67, 131).

27. Alfred Einstein, *A Short History of Music* (New York: Vintage Books, 1957), p. 94.

28. Arnold Dolmetsch, *The Interpretation of the Music of the XVII and XVIII Centuries* (London: Oxford University Press, 1946), p. 450.

29. Einstein, *Short History of Music*, p. 94.

30. Mann, Preface to *Stories*, p. vi; Friedman, *Stream of Consciousness*, p. 31; William York Tindall, *The Literary Symbol* (Bloomington: Indiana University Press, 1967), p. 263; David I. Grossvogel, *Limits of the Novel* (New York: Cornell University Press, 1968), p. 320.

## Chapter 2
### Form, Content, and the Process of Mind

1. Sterne to Dr. Eustace, 9 February 1768, *Letters*, p. 411.

2. Lodwick Hartley, *Laurence Sterne in the Twentieth Century*, (Chapel Hill: University of North Carolina Press, 1966), p. 69.

3. *Critical Review* 2 (April 1761): 316; Oliver Goldsmith, "The Citizen of the World," Letter Fifty-One, in *The Vicar of Wakefield and Other Writings*, ed. Frederick W. Hilles (New York: Random House, 1955), p. 159; Walpole to Dalrymple, 4 April 1760, *Letters of Horace Walpole*, 16 vols., ed. Mrs. Paget Toynbee (Oxford: Clarendon Press, 1903–1905), 4:369.

4. Walter Bagehot, "Sterne and Thackeray," *Literary Studies by Walter Bagehot*, 2 vols. (London and New York: J. M. Dent & E. P. Dutton, 1911), 2:105; E. M. Forster, *Aspects of the Novel* (New York: Harcourt, Brace, 1927), pp. 111–12. Arthur Calder-Marshall called *Tristram Shandy* "technically a hotch potch, without even the unity of mood in Burton's *Anatomy of Melancholy*," ("Laurence Sterne," *The English Novelists* [London: Chatto and Windus, 1936], p. 90). Walter Sichel called it "a farrago, a gallimaufry" (*Sterne*, p. 172), Ernest Baker "a salmigundi of odds and ends" ("The Intellectual Realism from Richardson to Sterne," *The History of the English Novel* [London: H. F. & G. Witherby, 1929–1930], 4: 244).

5. *A Later Pepys*, ed. Alice C. Gaussen (London and New York: J. Lane, 1904), 1: 219; *Monthly Review* 58 (January 1778): 85, 53; Traugott, *Tristram Shandy's World*, p. 124.

6. Laurence Sterne, *The Life and Opinions of Tristram Shandy, Gentleman*, ed. James Aiken Work (New York: Odyssey Press, 1940), 4:10.281. All future references to *Tristram Shandy* will be to this edition and will be contained in parentheses within the text. References are to volume, chapter, and page. See also: 1:14.36–37; 3:23.207; 6:6.416; 8:1.539; and 8:2.540. The gist of them all is, as Tristram says in the last, "I begin with writing the first sentence ——and trusting to Almighty God for the second."

7. 6:17.436 provides a nutritional explanation of the contrary methods:

> Now, when I write full,——I write as if I was never to write fasting again as long as I live;——that is, I write free from the cares, as well as the terrors of the world.——I count not the

number of my scars,——nor does my fancy go forth into dark
entries and bye corners to antedate my stabs.——In a word, my
pen takes its course; and I write on as much from the fullness of
my heart, as my stomach.——
    But when, an' please your honours, I indite fasting, 'tis a differ-
ent history.——I pay the world all possible attention and respect,
——and have as great a share (whilst it lasts) of that under-
strapping virtue of discretion, as the best of you.—— So that
betwixt both, I write a careless kind of a civil, nonsensical, good
humoured *Shandean* book, which will do all your hearts good——
——And all your heads too,——provided you understand it.

    8. See 2:4.91; 6:6.100; 9:12.614.
    9. Wayne Booth, *The Rhetoric of Fiction* (Chicago: University
of Chicago Press, 1961), pp. 229, 223–24.
    10. McKillop, *Early Masters of English Fiction*, p. 208. Although
more modest about the implications, others have also read the structure of the book as a reflection of the narrator's mind. "The assumption of Tristram's mind," Rufus Putney observes, "provides . . .
the chief structural device of the book" (Rufus Putney, "Laurence
Sterne, Apostle of Laughter," *Eighteenth Century English Literature: Modern  Essays in Criticism*, ed. James L. Clifford [New
York: Oxford University Press, 1959], p. 277). "'The history of
what passes in a man's own mind': that," writes Henri Fluchére, "is
what *Tristram Shandy* is. It is 'what passes in the mind' of Tristram
that provides the substance of the book, and it is *how* it passes that
gives it its structural unity—that is, the mind of Tristram at grips
with the data of his own reality, his person, his history, his temperament, his space and time, the people about him, the books he reads,
his ideas, his memories, and so on; but also the way he translates
into words this experience that he wishes to make us share rather
than just listen to" (Henri Fluchére, *Laurence Sterne From Tristram to Yorick*, trans. and abr. Barbara Bray [London: Oxford
University Press, 1965], pp. 86–87). And Samuel Monk sums it
up this way: "Locke gave him [Sterne] . . . a total view of the
mind of man, as well as the possibility of constructing a novel so as
to explore that mind. Instead of giving his tale a formal epic
structure, Sterne established the mind of the narrator, Tristram,
as the shaping force of the novel. The complexity of *Tristram
Shandy* is the complexity of the mind of man as Sterne perceived
it through Locke" (Introduction to *Tristram Shandy*, p. xi). Credit
for first pointing out this important Lockean influence on Sterne's
novel apparently belongs to Wilbur Cross.

11. Mark Schorer, "Technique as Discovery," *Hudson Review* 1 (1948): 67–87.

12. Ibid., p. 69.

13. Wayne Booth, "*Tristram Shandy* and Its Precursors" (Ph.D. diss., University of Chicago, 1950), p. 53n.

14. Ibid., p. 243.

15. Sterne to David Garrick, March 1762, *Letters*, p. 157; Denis Donoghue, "Sterne, Our Contemporary," *The Winged Skull*, p. 46; Northrop Frye, "Towards Defining an Age of Sensibility," *ELH* 23 (1956): 145.

16. Monroe Beardsley, *Aesthetics* (New York: Harcourt, Brace & World, 1958), p. 338; Roger Sessions, *The Musical Experience of Composer, Performer, Listener* (Princeton: Princeton University Press, 1950), p. 19; Schenker, Kurth, and Straus cited in Victor Zuckerkandl, *Sound and Symbol: Music and the External World*, trans. Willard Trask (New York: Pantheon Books, 1956), pp. 78–79. "It is, in fact, most striking with what uniformity, despite all differences between persons and periods, the idea of motion forced itself upon thinkers and scholars when the question of designating the essential element of music arose" (p. 77).

17. Thomas Munro, *Toward Science in Aesthetics* (New York: Bobbs-Merrill, 1956), pp. 20, 21–22.

18. For a discussion of the autonomous and heteronomous theories of music, see Leonard B. Meyer, *Emotion and Meaning in Music* (Chicago; University of Chicago Press, 1956), chapter 1; and Carroll Pratt, *The Meaning of Music* (New York: McGraw-Hill, 1931), pp. 205–20.

19. Eduard Hanslick, *The Beautiful in Music*, trans. Gustav Cohen, ed. Morris Weitz (New York: Bobbs-Merrill, 1957, originally published 1854), pp. 121–22.

20. Susanne Langer, *Philosophy in a New Key* (New York: Mentor Books, New American Library, 1948), pp. 178, 192.

21. James Beattie, *Essays on Poetry and Music, as They Affect the Mind; on Laughter, and Ludicrous Composition; on the Usefulness of Classical Learning*, 3rd ed. (London: E. and C. Dilly, 1779), pp. 120–21. By mid-eighteenth century, literal imitations of birds and bees and such were under scornful attack:

> The intention of Musick is not only to please the Ear, but to express the Sentiments, strike the Imagination, affect the Mind, and command the Passions. The Art of playing the Violin consists

in giving the Instrument a Tone that shall in a Manner rival the most perfect human Voice; . . . But as the imitating the Cock, Cuckoo, Owl, and other Birds . . . rather belong[s] to the Professors of Legerdemain and Posture-masters than to the Art of Music, the Lovers of that Art are not to expect to find anything of that Sort in this Book. (Francesco Geminiani, *The Art of Playing on the Violin*, London: Oxford University Press, 1751, p. 1.)

And J. A. Huller was even more contemptuous than Geminiani:

Our intermezzi . . . are full of fantastic imitations and silly tricks. There one can hear clocks striking, ducks jabbering, frogs quacking, and pretty soon one will be able to hear fleas sneezing and grass growing. ("Abhandlung von der Nachahmung der Natur in der Musik," in Marpurg's *Historischkritische Beytrage zur Aufnahme der Musik*, 5 vols. [1754–1760], 1:532. Cited in Langer, *Philosophy in a New Key*, p. 187.)

Still, even when music is being most diligently and foolhardily imitative, motion is likely to be crucial to the effort. Among the objects of imitation common to sixteenth- and seventeenth-century mimetic music were the Fall of Man, the Ascension of Christ, the "soaring" of birds, the "drifting" of rivers, the "turbulence" of brewing storms, and so on—all principally dependent on the motion of the music for their representation.

22. Charles Avison, *An Essay on Musical Expression*, 2nd ed. (London: C. Davis, 1753), p. 56.

23. Johann Nikolaus Forkel, *Musikalisch-Kritische Bibliothek*, Gotha, 1778, 1: 74. Cited in Paul Henry Lang, *Music in Western Civilization* (London: J. M. Dent & Sons, 1941), p. 588.

24. Leonard B. Meyer, "The Aesthetics of Stability," in *Music the Arts and Ideas* (Chicago: University of Chicago Press, 1967), p. 223.

25. Meyer, *Emotion and Meaning in Music*, pp. 35, 31.

26. Walter Pater, *The Renaissance* (New York: The Modern Library, n.d.; originally published 1873), pp. 111, 114.

27. Einstein, *Short History of Music*, pp. 93–94.

28. Thurston Dart, *The Interpretation of Music* (New York: Harper & Row, 1963), pp. 59–60, 63.

29. Lang, *Music in Western Civilization*, pp. 709, 537. "Similarly," Lang continues, "Buxtehude's, Reinken's, and Bach's improvisation of fugues and ciaconas was legendary. Improvisation on the organ and clavier remained a highly treasured art to Beethoven's time."

30. C.P.E. Bach, *Versuch über die wahre Art, des Clavier zu spielen*, in Oliver Strunk, *Source Readings in Music History* (New York: W. W. Norton, 1950), pp. 609–10.

31. Einstein, *Short History of Music*, p. 123.

32. From Blanchet's *Art du Chant*, cited in Meyer, *Emotion and Meaning in Music*, p. 206.

33. François Raguenet, "A Comparison Between the French and Italian Music" (anon. trans. ca. 1709), *Musical Quarterly* 32 (1946): 429.

34. Conrad Aiken, *Blue Voyage* (New York: Charles Scribner's Sons, 1927), pp. 291–92.

35. Aiken's review of his own *The Charnel Rose*, in *Poetry: A Magazine of Verse* 14 (1919): 152–59; Benjamin H. Lehman, "Of Time, Personality, and The Author," in *Laurence Sterne, A Collection of Critical Essays*, ed. John Traugott, (Englewood Cliffs, N.J.: Prentice Hall, 1968), p. 21.

36. Wolfgang Köhler, *Gestalt Psychology* (New York: Horace Liveright, 1929), pp. 248–59.

37. Conrad Aiken, *The Jig of Forslin*, 1:6.

38. Henri Bergson, *Le Rire* (Paris: Presses Universitaires, 1950), p. 115.

39. Langer, *Philosophy in a New Key*, p. 193.

40. Friedman, *Stream of Consciousness*, p. 126.

41. Wackenroder and Tieck, *Phantasien über die Kunst*, p. 115.

42. Hermann Hesse, *Betrachtungen, Gesammelte Dichtungen*, 4:113.

43. Ralph Freedman, *The Lyrical Novel*, p. 53.

## Chapter 3

### Simultaneity, Time, and the Art of Literary Counterpoint

1. Sessions, *The Musical Experience*, pp. 69–70.

2. See Wendell Johnson, "Browning's Music," *JAAC* 22 (1963): 206.

3. The best discussions of time in *Tristram Shandy* are the chapter on Sterne in Mendilow's *Time and the Novel*, pp. 158–99, Jean-Jacques Mayoux's "Laurence Sterne," in *Laurence Sterne*, ed. Traugott, pp. 108–25, and Mayoux's "Variations on the Time-sense

in *Tristram Shandy,*" *The Winged Skull,* pp. 3–18. I owe much to both Mendilow and Mayoux.

4. Joan Stambaugh, "Music as a Temporal Form," *Journal of Philosophy* 61 (1964): 276. Henri Bergson makes a similar point. For him, "real" time is not measurable, divisible clock time, but a psychological time, or "duration," that can only be lived and immediately apprehended. "The fact," writes Bergson, "is that, the further we penetrate into the depths of consciousness, the less right we have to treat psychic phenomena as things which are set side by side" (Henri Bergson, *Time and Free Will,* trans. F. L. Pogson [London: George Allen and Unwin], pp. 8–9). Psychological time is the survival of the no-longer-existent in the existent, the constant expansion of the existent by the addition of the not-yet-existent. It is continuous process, and its perfect image in the external world is music. See Zuckerkandl's discussion of Bergson on time in *Sound and Symbol,* p. 243. See also Bergson's *Matière et mémoire, Creative Evolution,* and *Durée et simultanéité.*

5. Christopher Simpson, *The Division Viol,* in Dolmetsch, *Interpretation of Music,* p. 329. Divisions may be homophonic or polyphonic. They are horizontal and polyphonic in the duet between Slop and Toby, divisions and fixed song interactive and complementary yet each carrying its own melody and going its own independent way. They are vertical and homophonic in Walter Shandy's divisions on the word *weakness,* where the divisions spin off from a single unmoving tone:

> For sure as ever the word *weakness* was uttered, and struck full upon his brain,——so sure it set him upon running divisions upon how many kinds of weaknesses there were;——that there was such a thing as weakness of the body,——as well as weakness of the mind,——and then he would do nothing but syllogize within himself for a stage or two together, How far the cause of all these vexations might, or might not, have arisen out of himself.
>
> In short, he had so many little subjects of disquietude springing out of this one affair, all fretting successively in his mind as they rose up in it, that my mother, whatever was her journey up, had but an uneasy journey of it down. (1:16.42–43)

Indeed, little subjects (often of disquietude) springing out of his affairs (often weaknesses), all fretting successively in his mind as they rise up in it, will not let Tristram alone either, and are responsible in no small measure for the rich contrapuntal (and harmonic) texture of his book.

6. For examples of contrapuntal dialogue, see 2:5.97–98; 5:10. 365; 6:18.437–38 (punctuated by rests); 7:34.526; 9:11.612–13, 613–14.

7. Mendilow, *Time and the Novel*, pp. 185–86.

8. "[My father] said his heart all along foreboded, and he saw it verified in . . . a thousand . . . observations he had made upon me, That I should neither think nor act like any other man's child: ——*But alas!* continued he, shaking his head a second time, and wiping away a tear which was trickling down his cheeks, *My Tristram's misfortunes began nine months before ever he came into the world*" (1:3.6–7).

9. Thomas Mann, *The Young Joseph*, p. 186, cited in Mendilow, *Time and the Novel*, p. 148.

10. Tristram's choice of terms here is interesting and I think significant. The term "rhapsody" or "rhapsodizing" was applied to both literary and musical composition, but more often to the latter. Bach used it synonymously with "fantasia": an irregular composition, following no strict style or form, usually consisting of familiar melodies arranged with frequent interludes and elaborate decorations. The fantasy, as we've said, is in many ways the closest musical analogue to *Tristram Shandy*.

11. This function was more common in later composition than in the medieval, where the invented melodies often bear scant relation to the borrowed *cantus firmus* tune.

12. Robert Erickson, *The Structure of Music* (New York: Noonday Press, 1957), p. 63.

13. Ibid., p. 201.

14. Felix Salzer, *Structural Hearing: Tonal Coherence in Music* (New York: Dover Publications, 1952), 2 volumes, 1:253.

15. See Aaron Copland, *What to Listen For in Music*, rev. ed. (New York: McGraw-Hill, 1963), p. 110.

## Chapter 4

### The Treatment of Themes:
### Exposition, Development, and Recapitulation

1. William York Tindall, *The Literary Symbol* (Bloomington: Indiana University Press, 1967), p. 49; Herbert J. Muller, *Modern Fiction: A Study of Values* (New York, Toronto, London: McGraw-Hill, 1937), p. 332.

2. Ford Madox Ford, *Provence*, 1935, p. 67. Cited in Mendilow, *Time and the Novel*, p. 55.

3. In his fine and thorough book, *Laurence Sterne From Tristram to Yorick*, Henri Fluchére pays considerable and acute attention to the peculiar thematic orientation and organization of *Tristram Shandy* and devotes almost one-third of his book to a chapter entitled "The Subject Matter and the Themes." The approach is suggestive, but Fluchére's view is that the interaction of the themes is haphazard and capricious.

> Against the background of the absurd . . . which gives the book its atmosphere and ambience, the good-natured hobby-horses gallop or amble along, while the most varied themes intersect in an apparently disordered network of which the pattern and rhythm defy description. In virtue of the same principles that govern the structure of *Tristram Shandy*, the sequence of themes, like the sequence of events cannot be accounted for in terms of logic, much as the critic might wish it. The themes are linked to episodes and characters, and among themselves, but their interdependence is not always clear because it is subject to the intellectual structure of the book as a whole. They crop up here and there in fragments of very unequal importance without being developed to their conclusions; they are abandoned, resumed, set aside again only to reappear again further on, sometimes much further on, and their reappearance does not necessarily have anything to do with a rational order. (Fluchére, pp. 147–48)

The difference between us should be clear. In my view the pattern and rhythm, while at times surely haphazard and indefinable, can also often be described in musical terms, and the interdependence of the themes is clearer than Fluchére allows because subject to the musical structure of the book as a whole; the intellectual structure *is* musical, and therein lies the order and describability.

4. And again,

> I have been the continual sport of what the world calls fortune; and though I will not wrong her by saying, She has ever made me feel the weight of any great or signal evil;——yet with all the good temper in the world, I affirm it of her, that in every stage of my life, and at every turn and corner where she could get fairly at me, the ungracious Duchess has pelted me with a set of as pitiful misadventures and cross accidents as ever small HERO sustained. (1:5.10)

5. Mrs. Shandy's question is, ominously, an interruption. The digressions on time in the novel are likewise interruptions of a kind, intrusions into the tale Tristram has ostensibly set out to tell

and icons of the very problem they raise: the incompatibility of clock and psychological time and the unreceptivity of chronology and time to the constant intrusions and diversions the fullest truth demands. Nor are these the only interruptions. They are everywhere, the mark of his eccentric method and the soul of his work, and they owe their presence to the interruption that began it all.

6. *Harvard Dictionary of Music*, 2d ed., Willi Apel (Cambridge, Mass.: Harvard University Press, 1969); entry under *Development*, p. 229.

7. Ibid.

8. Mitford to Sir William Elford, 13 May 1815, *Letters of Mary Russell Mitford*, ed. Brimley Johnson, cited in Mendilow, *Time and the Novel*, p. 167.

9. Incidentally (or not) the same habit of association that biologically assured his personal eccentricity likewise contributes formally to the perverseness of his work.

10. Sessions, *The Musical Experience*, pp. 55–56.

11. Alec Robertson and Denis Stevens, *Pelican History of Music*, 3 vols. (Harmondsworth, Middlesex: Penguin Books, 1960), 3:56.

12. Sessions, *The Musical Experience*, p. 58.

13. Aldous Huxley, *Point Counter Point* (Modern Library: New York; Copyright 1928, Doubleday Doran,), pp. 349–50.

14. I am indebted for these observations on the rise of tonality and homophony to Manuel F. Bukofzer, *Music of the Baroque Period* (London: J. M. Dent & Sons, 1947), pp. 219–25.

15. The idea for such correspondences, Bukofzer notes, goes back to the speculative theory of antiquity which connected the tones with the planets, and planets in turn with the various states of mind and soul. (Ibid., pp. 365–66).

16. Sir John Hawkins, *A General History of the Science and Practice of Music*, 2 vols. (New York: J. L. Peters, 1875 [orig. pub. 1776]), 1:59, 60.

17. Huxley, *Point Counter Point*, p. 350.

18. Monk, Introduction to *Tristram Shandy*, pp. xv, xvi.

19. John M. Stedmond, *The Comic Art of Laurence Sterne* (Toronto: University of Toronto Press, 1967), p. 90.

20. The original version, Work informs us, ended: ". . . in which it has ever been my purpose to pass from jests to worthy seriousness." The alteration indicates Sterne's prevailing interest in constant movement and transition, in process rather than arrival, even at "worthy seriousness."

21. Ernest Nevin Dilworth, *The Unsentimental Journey of Laurence Sterne* (New York: King's Crown Press, 1948).

22. John W. Draper, "Poetry and Music in Eighteenth Century Aesthetics," *Englische Studien* 67 (1932), p. 85. In "The Remarkable Musical Life of the Musician Joseph Berglinger" (1795), Wackenroder wrote: "At other times again, the music called forth a wondrous blend of gladness and sadness in his heart, so that he was equally inclined to smile and weep—a mood we meet so often on our way through life, for whose expression there is no fitter art than music" (Oliver Strunk, *Source Readings in Musical History*, p. 754).

23. Johann Joachim Quantzens (Quantz), *Versuch einer Anweisung die Flöte traversiere zu spielen* (Berlin: Johann Friedrich Voss, 1752), p. 110, cited in Dolmetsch, *Interpretation of Music*, p. 25.

24. Daniel Webb, *Observations on the Correspondence Between Poetry and Music* (London: J. Dodsley, 1769), pp. 47–48.

25. Ibid., p. 50.

26. Herbert Read, preface to *A Sentimental Journey* (Scholartis Press, 1929).

27. Pratt, *Meaning of Music*, p. xxv.

28. *Pelican History of Music*, 3:21, 43–44.

29. Lang, *Music in Western Civilization*, p. 590.

30. Einstein, *Short History of Music*, p. 96.

31. What these perplexities of my uncle Toby were,———'tis impossible for you to guess;———if you could,———I should blush, not as a relation,———not as a man,———nor even as a woman, ———but I should blush as an author; inasmuch as I set no small store by myself upon this very account, that my reader has never yet been able to guess at any thing. And in this, Sir, I am of so nice and singular a humour, that if I thought you was able to form the least judgment or probably conjecture to yourself, of what was to come in the next page,———I would tear it out of my book. (1:25.80)

32. *Pelican History of Music*, 3:49.

33. Lang, *Music in Western Civilization*, p. 594.

34. Marcia Allentuck, "In Defense of an Unfinished *Tristram Shandy:* Laurence Sterne and the *Non Finito*," *The Winged Skull*, pp. 145–46.

35. E. M. Forster, *Aspects of the Novel* (New York: Harcourt, Brace, 1927), pp. 168–69.

36. Donald Francis Tovey, *The Forms of Music* (Cleveland: World, 1956), p. 220.

37. For two discussions of the limits of repetition in the arts see Zuckerkandl, *Sound and Symbol*, pp. 212–23, and Brown, *Music and Literature*, pp. 103–13. Zuckerkandl finds the root of music's circularity in the octave itself. In the system of the scales,

> The tone toward which we look in the descending segment of the curve is always the same tone we left behind us in its ascending segment. We go toward a tone by going away from it. The distance in pitch from the point of departure increases with every step, but with the eighth tone we are again at the point of departure. Leaving has become returning; start has become goal.
>
> This is the phenomenon that has fittingly been called "the miracle of the octave"; Ernst Kurth characterizes it as "one of the greatest riddles . . . the beginning of irrationality in music, a thing unparalleled in all the rest of the phenomenal world." (p. 102)

38. A number of these gathered threads were first pointed out by Wayne Booth, "Did Sterne Complete Tristram Shandy?," *Modern Philology* 48 (1951): 172–83, and Overton Philip James, *The Relation of Tristram Shandy to the Life of Sterne* (The Hague: Mouton, 1966), chap. 6, pp. 129–61.

39. Booth, "Did Sterne Complete Tristram Shandy?," p. 182.

40. Ibid.

41. James, *Relation of Tristram Shandy*, pp. 154–55.

42. Booth, "Did Sterne Complete Tristram Shandy?," p. 181.

43. Gide, *The Counterfeiters*, pt. 2, chap. 3, 168–69. For an insightful discussion of *The Counterfeiters*, to which I'm indebted, see Wallace Fowlie, *André Gide: His Life and Art* (New York: Macmillan Co. 1965), pp. 85–97.

# Chapter 5

## Concentricity: Wheels Within Wheels

1. From the Preface to Cadilhac's *La pastorale* (Paris, 1924). Cited in Brown, *Music and Literature*, p. 174.

2. *A Sentimental Journey* still more than *Tristram Shandy*. The *Journey* fairly bristles with musical images, similes, and terminology. There are, in fact, forty-six references to music in this small book—in a standard text about one every third page. Of these, thirty-two are literal references—trips to concerts and the *opera*

*comique*, encounters with country dancers and musicians, episodes involving singing, piping, dancing and the like—while fourteen are figurative, e.g., "La Fleur, whose heart seem'd only to be tuned to joy," or "it was touching a cold key with a flat third to it, upon the close of a piece of music, which had call'd forth my affections." The result, as Cadilhac predicts, is a distinctly musical atmosphere, the purpose of which, in *A Sentimental Journey*, seems to be primarily to emphasize and enrich the novel's sentimentalism.

3. Strictly defined, a dance, though it usually is, need not be "musical" or accompanied by music. Sterne's use and exploitation of the metaphor, however, together with the descriptions of actual dances in volume 7 indicate that the dance and dances he has in mind are musically conceived and accompanied. See also 8:1.539.

4. Similarly, looking into his father's equally excursive mind, Tristram exclaims: "tormenting world! which led his imagination a thorny dance, and, before all was over, play'd the duce and all with him" (1:16.42).

5. For additional examples in volume 7, and there are many, see 7.487; 10.491; 15.495–96; 17.498–99; 19.502; 42.534.

6. The chapter is too long to be reproduced in the text, but its thorough musical saturation makes it well worth quoting in its entirety. To pick up where the text leaves off, the passage proceeds as follows:

There is nothing in playing before good judges,——but there's a man there——no——not him with the bundle under his arm ——the grave man in black.——'Sdeath! not the gentleman with the sword on.——Sir, I had rather play a *Caprichio* to *Calliope* herself, then draw my bow across my fiddle before that very man; and yet, I'll stake my *Cremona* to a *Jew*'s trump, which is the greatest musical odds that ever were laid, that I will this moment stop three hundred and fifty leagues out of tune upon my fiddle, without punishing one single nerve that belongs to him.——Twaddle diddle, tweddle diddle,——twiddle diddle, ——twoddle diddle,——twuddle diddle,——prut-trut——krish ——krash——krush.——I've undone you, Sir,——but you see he is no worse,——and was *Apollo* to take his fiddle after me, he can make him no better.

Diddle diddle, diddle diddle, diddle diddle——hum——dum ——drum.

——Your worships and your reverences love musick——and God has made you all with good ears——and some of you play delightfully yourselves——trut-prut,——prut-trut.

O! there is——whom I could sit and hear whole days,—— whose talents lie in making what he fiddles to be felt,——who inspires me with his joys and hopes, and puts the most hidden springs of my heart into motion.——If you would borrow five guineas of me, Sir,——which is generally ten guineas more than I have to spare——or you, Messrs. Apothecary and Taylor, want your bills paying,——that's your time. (371–72)

7. In Schenkerian analysis an entire musical composition may be the artistic elaboration or unfolding of a single chord. "The structural outline or framework [often embodied in a single tonic triad (I-V-I, I-II-V-I, I-III-V-I, or I-IV-V-I)] represents the fundamental motion to the goal; it shows the direct, the shortest way to this goal. The whole interest and tension of a piece consists in the expansions, modifications, detours and elaborations of this basic direction, and these we call the prolongations" (Felix Salzer, *Structural Hearing: Tonal Coherence in Music*, 2 vols. [New York: Dover, 1952], 1:14).

8. Copland, *What to Listen For in Music*, p. 79.

9. Ibid.

10. "[T]he principle of the fifth and of the third not only affects the form in so far as the extension of an individual idea or even a group of ideas is concerned, but affects the form in so far as form is the sum total of all ideas brought to interplay, i.e., the form of the whole. We see how in most cyclic compositions the content is developed from the starting point of the main key to that of the dominant: the complex of the subsidiary section and that of the closing section, i.e., the second and third thematic complexes, are usually set in the key of the dominant. On the other hand, the recapitulation brings an inversion from the dominant back to the tonic. Most compositions in the major mode take this turn. . . . [The layman] speaks of a so-called 'classical form' as if it were something stabilized; he speaks of a 'sonata form,' a 'symphonic form,' etc., as if, e.g., all sonatas were the same merely because their harmonic development often moves from the tonic to the dominant, etc. Instead of recognizing in this a feature of Nature, which cannot be rejected by any genius but can at most be replaced at certain times by modifying surrogates; instead of understanding that Nature must penetrate all forms of music—be they sonatas or waltzes, symphonies or potpourris—the layman will mistake the command of Nature for a quality of form!" (Heinrich Schenker, *Harmony* [Chicago: University of Chicago Press, 1954; originally published in 1906 as *New Musical Theories and Fantasies—by an Artist*], pp. 246–47, 250).

11. See Schenker's *Harmony*, particularly sections 115 ff, and Oswald Jonas's Introduction, pp. v–xxiv.

12. Salzer, *Structural Hearing*, 1:246. Salzer makes specific reference to three-part composition here, but the point is by no means restricted to compositions of this kind. Schenker himself rejected the narrow historic definition of sonata or symphonic form and traced the principle and implications of *Auskomponierung* back to Bach and the early eighteenth century. Salzer has extended it back to Monteverdi and Frescobaldi and forward to Prokofieff, Copland, and Vaughan Williams.

13. The marbled page, "(motley emblem of my work!)," the black page that mystically hides so many opinions, transactions, and truths beneath its dark veil, and the illustrated and infinitely suggestive rhetorical flourish of Trim's stick are more nearly analogous to the chord. They are all in effect emblems of the total work, of its preoccupation with the visual (indeed with the emblematic), with expression, sign, and gesture, and emblems of the major themes of confusion, motley, hidden implications, and affective communication.

14. "What I have to inform you, comes, I own, a little out of its due course;——for it should have been told a hundred and fifty pages ago, but that I foresaw then 'twould come in pat hereafter, and be of more advantage here than elsewhere.——Writers had need look before them to keep up the spirit and connection of what they have in hand.

When these two things are done,——the curtain shall be drawn up again, and my uncle *Toby*, my father, and Dr. *Slop* shall go on with their discourse, without any more interruption" (2:19.144–45).

15. Copland, *What to Listen For in Music*, p. 83.

16. From the definition of *Form* in *Grove's Dictionary of Music and Musicians*, 5th ed., ed. Eric Blom (London: Macmillan, 1954), 3:429.

17. Brown, *Music and Literature*, pp. 108–9.

18. Zuckerkandl, *Sound and Symbol*, p. 219.

19. See, for example, 5:7.359–60: "He is dead"; 6:6–7.417–19: uncle Toby's pipe; 8:35.594 and 9:1.599: "And look through the key-hole as long as you will"; 9:11.612: "'Now what can their two noddles be about?' cried my father."

20. The face alone may also be a musical instrument, and Phutatorius's is as expressive as Walter's:

So that notwithstanding he looked with all the attention in the world, and had gradually skrewed up every nerve and muscle in his face, to the utmost pitch the instrument would bear, in order, as it was thought, to give a sharp reply to *Yorick*, who sat over-against him——Yet I say, was *Yorick* never once in any one domicile of *Phutatorius's* brain——but the true cause of his exclamation lay at least a yard below. (4:27.319)

21. Cited in Margaret Shaw's Introduction to the (spurious) *Second Journal to Eliza* (London: George Bell & Sons, 1929), p. xxviii. Shaw, it turns out, is probably wrong about the authenticity of the *Second Journal*, but her argument for its attribution to Sterne is largely, almost exclusively in terms of the musicality of its prose:

> The delicate sequence of light-stressed, high-pitched vowels, proceeding on an almost imperceptibly rising rhythm, gives to the opening phrases the character of an *Adagio* movement, and indicates, behind the simple statement of the idea, a mood of resigned and pensive melancholy. As the phrases pass from statement with an undercurrent of feeling to the more direct expression of emotion the measure changes, and, still in rising rhythm, but with swifter turns of phrase and with more stress on the accented syllables, breaks up into 'short swallow-flights of song', to return again to the opening mood, and so proceeds to the last cadence with its sonorous closing chord. . . . In the continuity of its rhythmical pattern,—which contains no modulation, tonality or cadence foreign to Sterne,—[the *Second Journal*] makes good its claim to be considered an authentic work.

And again,

> How graciously smooth is each phrase in this *pastorale!* From its antiphonal opening, thru the subtly beautiful divisions of the second movement, to its quiet close on a repetition of the original phrasing, an unbroken melody binds together all its subtle variations of tone. This is, indeed, the most exquisite harmony of music and meaning. . . .
> In methods of composition, then, the *Second Journal* is in keeping with all that we know of Sterne. So, too, is the personality of its writer. The same whimsical juxtaposition of humour and pathos, the same swift and even startling transitions of thought and mood, the same minute notation of expression and gesture which makes Sterne's manner so inimitable. (pp. xv–xvi, xix, xxxi)

Not quite. Sterne's prose is imitable and was imitated (well enough to fool Ms. Shaw), probably, as Lewis Curtis shows, by William Combe ["Forged Letters of Laurence Sterne," *PMLA* 50 (1935): 1076–1106]. What is of interest here, though, is first that Shaw defends her attribution on these grounds; second that what she says about Combe's imitation is far more subtly but no less true of Sterne's own prose (she is, after all, basing her claim on a comparison with *Tristram Shandy*, *A Sentimental Journey*, the letters, and the authentic *Journal to Eliza*, and her ear, while not sensitive to subtle nuance is keen to sound); third that Combe picked up and exaggerated the musical flow, contours, transitions, and cadences of Sterne's style; and finally that he helped his hoax along with a generous sprinkling—too generous and so suspicious—of elaborate musical metaphors.

22. Fluchére, *Laurence Sterne*, p. 421.

23. Monk, xix.

24. When the rest is longer than a mere dash could reasonably suggest, Tristram indicates the pauses verbally, at times their precise length. See, for example, 6:18.437–38 for a typically strained, contrapuntal, and repetitive exchange between Walter and Elizabeth.

25. Beattie, *Essays on Poetry and Music*, p. 281.

26. The entire chapter is permeated with music, both as metaphor and as literal presence.

27. Locke, *Essay Concerning Human Understanding*, 3:2.2.

28. Fluchére, *Laurence Sterne*, p. 403.

29. Robert Bridges, "On the Musical Setting of Poetry," in *Collected Essays, Papers, &c.*, 2 vols. (London: Oxford University Press, 1927), 2:1–13.

# Index